Chandra Naadi
(Part - 2)

An Expounding Version

Tirupur S. Gopalakrishnan (GK)

Translated by Sethumadhavan Venkatrao

ISBN 979-8-89519-818-6

Sri Uchista Maha Ganapathaye Namah:

Submitted at the Lotus feet of my Living God

Guruji Shri. Tirupur S. Gopalakrishnan (GK)

Dedication

I offer my humble prayers

To

My Parents

Who have

Parented Me

And

Raised me up

Considering my development

As their own

Bless me Dad

Bless me Mom

Contents

Prayer

Let us submit our prayers to

Our mother

Our Father

Those who were our preceptors and pedagogues till now by touching their lotus feet

Our family deity

Our tutelary God

Our chosen God

Guardian deity

Special/specific deities of the residential town

Let mystics, saints, gurus, spiritual heads, eminent astrologers, the five elements, nature, stellar constellation, the zodiac, the planets, and omnipresent power bless us.

Let our word, actions, and deeds not hurt or hinder people's progress.

Let peace prevail with all.

Sri Uchista Maha Ganapathaye Namah!

Sri Uchista Maha Ganapathaye Namah!

Sri Uchista Maha Ganapathaye Namah!

At the start of every class, I always offer my prayers along the above lines.

I bestow this prayer to everybody.

Prayers to Preceptor

I at this moment submit my humble prayers to my father who is also my first preceptor in astrology

Late **Shri. N. Selvarasu Pillai for** giving me love, education, pleasure, enlightenment, and knowledge

To my Guru Late Shri. Guru Rama Subbu

To my Guru who leads me in absentia Late Shri. K. S. Krishnamurthy (K.S.K)

I humbly pray to all saints, spiritual Gurus, Rishis, and the astrological fraternity.

My greetings to my fellow astrologers.

Seeking the blessings of all

Tirupur S. Gopalakrishnan (GK)

Thanks Note

Sree Uchishta Maha Ganapathy Namah

This book was published in Tamil and received attention and appreciation from all.

I humbly thank my mentor and guide of all time Dr K Nataraj P.hd., (Astro), Oddanchathiram.

I take this opportunity to thank Guruji Shri L. Duraiswamy, Headmaster (Retd) and honorary President of Gurunathar Nadi Astrology Centre.

I would like to thank the Admin of GK Foundation Ms Aswini K. Thangalakshmi – Sankarankoil for her efforts in the propagation of my astrological thoughts to all through our Foundation.

I also take this opportunity to express my sincere thanks to:

Mr Sankar and MrsTamizharasi Sankar

Sri D. Balakrishnan – Axe Oil, Chennai,

Sri R. Sakthivel – Ayyappa Label,

Sri. M. M. Kumarasamy, Sri. G. N. Palanivel, Sri. G. S. Shanmugasundaram

Sri P. R. Selvaganesh – Bangalore for being the reason for my many books in many languages,

My well-wisher Sri Aditya Guruji – Chennai.

Mr Sethumadhavan Venkatrao, Chennai for translating this book into English.

I must also thank

Sri S. Suresh – Coimbatore,

Sri B. Senthil Kumar – Tirupur, all the GK Astro Admin executives for their tireless support to me.

My sincere thanks to the management, executives, and staff of Notion Press for bringing up this book in a fitting manner.

I convey my heartfelt thanks and blessings to everyone.

– Tirupur S. Gopalakrishnan (GK)

9842220903

gkastro.tirupur@gmail.com

About the Book

I am thrilled to note that my brainchild 'Chandra Naadi' has grown to an adult age from the day of its first publication in 2007. It is my strong notion that unless an astrologer foresees the purpose for which a client has approached him, he could never see a smile on his client's face. My past experiences in such situations kept urging me to look for a solution to gauge the purpose of the approach of my clients. I have spent 3 years analysing the charts of those who had come to me and finally arrived at the conclusion that **the Moon in transit** kindles the mind of the people to look for some solution for the crisis caused by planets in transit when they are about to conjoin (before and after), aspect the planets posited in their natal (birth) chart including their positions.

To put it simply, it is ideal to predict based on the transit Moon's connections with planets in the natal (birth) chart instead of hovering over all the planets. I have classified the considerations under six headings as under.

1. **The Moon of the day of consultation represents the questioner/Client.**
2. **Natal Planets that conjoin or aspect the Moon indicate the problems/crisis of the questioner/Client at present.**
3. **The problems already faced by the questioner/Client Are indicated by the planets which the Moon has crossed over.**
4. **The problems the questioner/Client is about to face are indicated by the Moon to meet/approach next.**
5. **Planets posited in trines (1, 5, 9) to the transit Moon reveal the future incidents awaiting the questioner/Client to face.**
6. **What is the present position of the transiting planet that indicates the problem being faced by the questioner/Client?**

The status of the above six positions is the thumb rule to arrive at the predictions.

My research clearly emphasises the complete, clear and thorough knowledge of the Karakathuvas of Sign/Rasi and Bhava, benefic and malefic results of the association/aspect of Planets and their conjunctions, and planetary transit movements before declaring the results to the querist/Client.

I am very happy to announce the publication of this book in FOUR Volumes and FOUR Languages viz. English, Hindi, and Kannada along with this Tamil edition. This book has been taken up for research by one of my female students and submitted as a thesis to the University. Thousands of astrologers are using 'Chandra Naadi's rules in their predictions and their success thrills me. I believe all these happenings are the choicest blessings showered on me by my Lord Sri Uchishta Maha Ganapathy (Ganesha) who is the guiding factor of my inner self.

In the Service of God…
– Tirupur S. Gopalakrishnan (GK)

Some Reminiscences from 'Chandra Naadi'
First Version

The very success of 'Chandra Naadi' is its simple rules and easy application. There are no major violations or deviations from the rules of original scriptures and treatises formulated by Great Saints and Rishis like Parashara and Varhamihira. I have not taken Maharishi Jaimini's school of thought (**Jaimini Sutras governing side aspects**) into consideration in this book. In addition to its simplicity, the special feature and beauty are that even very minute problems can be identified through 'Chandra Naadi' and solutions to the same can be suggested.

It is an essential factor that the basics of astrology – the five essences (Pancha-anga) of the almanack, Karakathuvas of Rasi and Bhavas, friendly, neutral and enmity between planets along with their positional strength and weakness at the point of exaltation and debilitation, their impact during conjunction and aspect of one another, occupation of the asterisms of other planets, in same Divisions, and transit including their Maha Dasa (Dasa), Anthar Dasa (Bukthi), and Prithyanthar Dasa (Antharam) should be well known and understood with its implications before attempting to predict using all methods of astrology including 'Chandra Naadi'.

I have reiterated the necessity of strong knowledge about the astrological basics of planets as 'Chandra Naadi' is written based on the fact that planets impart their results through their aspects of a sign or the planets posited in the sign to act. While the association of friendlier planets extend good benefic results, planets with enmity amongst them give malefic results to the native pushing him to face problems. Positioning of the planets in trines (1, 5, 9) or squares (1, 4, 7, 10) to each other intensifies or reduces the benefic or malefic results depending on their friendlier, neutral or inimical nature. One more consideration concerning the trines (1, 5, 9) is the implication of Drekkana positions (Divisional Chart 3 – position of planets in 0 – 10, 10 – 20, or 20 – 30 degrees in a sign) exhibiting their impactful nature at 100% in 0 – 10 degrees, 60% in 20 – 30 degrees and 40% when positioned in 20 – 30 degrees from each other. E.g. Let us consider a planet posited at 5° in Aries and find another planet at 0 – 10 degrees in Leo or Sagittarius. These two are considered to be 100% strong trine Lords. If the other planet is positioned between 10 – 20 degrees in Leo or Sagittarius the strength will be 60% and further reduced to 40% when placed between 20 – 30 degrees in Leo or Sagittarius while the primary planet in Aries remains at 5 degrees.

Lord of Obstacles (Bhathagathipathi)

Obstacles (Bathakathipathi/Evil) Signs of the Zodiac

The ascendants are classified as 1. Chara (cardinal or movable) 2. Sthira (Fixed or Stable) and 3. Ubaya (Dual or both movable and fixed).

For Chara (Cardinal) ascendant, the 11th house is the Obstacle/Bathaka (affliction) Sign/Rasi.

For the Fixed (Sthira) ascendant, the 9th house is the Obstacle/Bathaka (affliction) Sign/Rasi

For Ubaya (Dual) ascendant the 7th house is the Obstacle/Bathaka (affliction) Sign/Rasi

Trouble mongers

For Chara ascendant, the 11th house lord and planets posited in the 11th house is the Lord of Obstacles (Bathakathipathi)

For the Fixed (Sthira) ascendant, the 9th house lord and planets posited in the 9th house is the Lord of Obstacles (Bathakathipathi).

For the Ubaya (Dual) ascendant, the 7th house lord and planets posited in the 7th house is the Lord of Obstacles (Bathakathipathi)

Inimical Planets only extend their evil effects through the Lord of Obstacles (Bathakathipathi/troublemongers). Hence predictions should be given after taking the Lord of Obstacles (Bathakathipathi's) status in the zodiac.

The troubles between stationed Planets should be reckoned when they are in positions 6 and 8 from each other, as for the ascendant.

Ashtamathipathi or the Lord of the 8th House

For each ascendant, its 8th house lord will be reckoned as Ashtamathipathi. The Lord of the 8th house/Ashtamathipathi and Planets posited in the 8th house give trouble, loss, and grief to the native through his/her greediness.

Ashtamathipathi showers his blessings through treasure when the native is not greedy. At the same time, he gives obstacles and grief when the native is greedy.

The position of the 8th house lord should be taken into account by the ascendant as well from each planet. Ashtamathipathi from the ascendant will be the primary trouble creator.

Ashtamathipathi from each planet will afflict that particular planet only.

Twenty-Seven Asterisms

(STARS)

1 to 9	9 to 18	19 to 27	Star-Lord	Maha Dasa Period (years)
Aswini	Magha	Moola	Ketu	7
Barani	Poorva-phalguni	Poorva-Ashada	Venus	20
Krittika	Uttara-phalguni	Uttara-Ashada	Sun	6
Rohini	Hastha	Shravana	Moon	10
Mrigsira	Chitra	Dhanishta	Mars	7
Arudra	Swathi	Satabhisha	Rahu	18
Punarvasu	Vishaka	Poorva-Bhadra	Jupiter	16
Pushyami	Anuradha	Uttara-Bhadra	Saturn	19
Aslesha	Jyestha	Revathi	Mercury	17

The above table shows the twenty-seven asterisms (stars) and their respective Dasa lords and Dasa period which should be remembered.

The moon's distancing at 0° to 180° from the Sun is termed a Waxing Moon (Sukla Paksha) gaining strength and its moving away from 180° of the Sun is termed a Waning Moon (Krishna Paksha) losing strength. Waxing Moon is considered as benefic while it is considered malefic while waning.

Nine Planets:

Two luminaries the Sun and the Moon. Five planets – Mars, Mercury, Jupiter, Venus, and Saturn. The two nodes termed shadow planets are Rahu and Ketu.

Planetary aspects and control:

9 Planets	Aspect or Control
Ketu	Controls 3, 11 houses
Venus	Aspect 7th house
Sun	Aspect 7th house
Moon	Aspect 7th house
Mars	Aspect 4th, 7th and 8th house
Rahu	Controls 3, 11 houses
Jupiter	Aspect 5th, 7th, and 9th house
Saturn	Aspect 3rd, 7th, and 10th house
Mercury	Aspect 7th house

Pisces (Meena) Exaltation – Venus Debilitation – Mercury Ruler – Jupiter 330° – 360°	Aries (Mesha) Exaltation – Sun Debilitation – Saturn Ruler – Mars 0° – 30°	Taurus (Rishabha) Exaltation – Moon Debilitation – None Ruler – Venus 30° – 60°	Gemini (Mithuna) Exaltation – None Debilitation – None Ruler – Mercury 60° – 90°
Aquarius (Kumbha) Exaltation – None Debilitation – None Ruler – Saturn 300° – 330°	**Exaltation Debilitation Ruling Status Of Planets**		Cancer (Kataka) Exaltation – Jupiter Debilitation – Mars Ruler – Moon 90° – 120°
Capricorn (Makara) Exaltation – Mars Debilitation – Jupiter Ruler – Saturn 270° – 300°			Leo (Simma) Exaltation – None Debilitation – None Ruler – Sun 120° – 150°
Sagittarius (Dhanus) Exaltation – None Debilitation – None Ruler – Jupiter 240° – 270°	Scorpio (Viruchiga) Exaltation – None Debilitation – Moon Ruler – Mars 210° – 240°	Libra (Thula) Exaltation – Saturn Debilitation – Sun Ruler – Venus 180° – 210°	Virgo (Kanya) Exaltation – Mercury Debilitation – Venus Ruler – Mercury 150° – 180°

A planet debilitates in the 7th house (opposite of) its house of exaltation. Gemini (Mithuna), Leo (Simma), Sagittarius (Dhanus), and Aquarius (Kumbha) find no exalted or debilitated in them. When the question of debilitation or exaltation of the nodes Rahu/Ketu arises, my answer is negative.

Friendliness and Enmity of Planets:

It is more important to know the Planets' friendlier and envious nature to assess the results during the planetary transit.

Planet	Enemy Planets
Sun	Saturn, Rahu, Ketu
Moon	Rahu, Ketu
Mars	Mercury, Saturn, Rahu, Ketu
Mercury	Moon, Mars, Rahu, Ketu
Jupiter	Rahu, Ketu
Venus	Rahu, Ketu
Saturn	Mars, Rahu, Ketu
Rahu	All Planets
Ketu	All Planets

The above positions of planets are adopted in this book.

Transit and Medical Treatment

Pisces (Meena) Feet Eyes	Aries (Mesha) Head Brain	Taurus (Rishabha) Neck Glands Thyroid Eyes Face	Gemini (Mithuna) Skin Hands Fingers Shoulders
Aquarius (Kumbha) Anklets Blood Breathing	Kalapursha (Time personified) pointers to identify disease		Cancer (Kataka) Respiratory Organs Chest Heart blood circulation
Capricorn (Makara) Knee Joints			Leo (Simma) Stomach Heart Large intestine Naval (Umbilical cord)
Sagittarius (Dhanus) Thighs Heart valves Artery	Scorpio (Viruchiga) Uterus Rectum Anus	Libra (Thula) Kidney	Virgo (Kanya) Abdomen Back Spine Smaller intestine Hip

While declaring the disease based on Kalapurusha (Time personified), it will be easy to identify the affected part of the body and the extent of affliction.

Operations/Surgeries should not be carried out on the parts of the body denoted by the Rasi/sign over which *the Transit Moon* is passing. As our body contains more fluids and is the lord of fluids, the Moon indicates the nature of the parts of the body.

An astrologer with his exceptional knowledge in asterisms (stars), drekkana (decanates), and sign theories can act as a Doctor/

Physician as in the olden days a physician acted as an astrologer and vice versa.

Example:

Stomach/large intestine/naval/umbilical cord-related Surgeries/operations should not be undertaken when the transit Moon passes over the Leo/Simma sign.

Abdomen, uterus, and rectum-related surgeries/operations should not be carried out while the Moon transits over Scorpio/viruchiga Rasi/sign. If surgeries/operations are undertaken the disease will not get cured easily in full and its back effects will remain for a longer period and at times throughout life. Diseases indicated in the parts of the body represented in the *Kalapurusha* (Timer personified) will reflect in the Lagna/ascendant signified parts of the body.

Based on the Planets in the natal chart...

1. The natural character of the native
2. The income sources destined/entitled by the native
3. The lifestyle/circle of the native should be ascertained

Based on the transit Planets...

a) Is there a change in the character/tendencies of the native
b) The present income status/financial sources
c) Is there any radical change at present in the financial conditions of the native

Based on the Maha Dasa (Dasa), Anthar Dasa (Bukthi)...

A) What are the events to occur and when?
B) What is the intensity of the event?
C) Whether the native stands to gain or lose due to the event.

The results of the transit will be short-lived and temporary whereas those from the Maha Dasa (Dasa) and Anthar Dasa (Bukthi) will be permanent and long-lasting. While the transit indicates ailments of shorter durations, chronic diseases and medicines for a lifetime are indicated by the Maha Dasa (Dasa) and Anthar Dasa (Bukthi). To declare the transit results, planetary positions will be more appropriate than bhavagas. Maha Dasa (Dasa) and Anthar Dasa (Bukthi) will cause their effects to be based on bhavagas and predictions based on bhavagas will be more precise than that of planetary positions.

Planetary Combinations

Below are a few resultants but not limited to the planetary combinations or their aspects over the same sign they are posited in the natal (birth) chart of a native. These basic effects should be co-related during their transit in line with the transit Moon, the revelation of 'Chandra Naadi'.

Sun + Moon

- Both parents will lead a harmonious and affectionate life.
- The mother will agree and adopt in tune with the father.
- The Mother will manage the family.
- Affliction to the eye may be felt.
- The father will be fickle-minded and may be a frequent traveller.

There will be frequent behavioural changes because of the Sun + Moon combination in a Sign which is considered a boon or fortune as 'Full Moon' or 'Pournami Yoga' in treatises, slimmer as it starts waning the effects of which can be felt in transit.

Sun + Mars

- The body temperature of the native will always be high.
- In a fit of rage, he will quit or resign his job all of a sudden.
- His angry temperament shoots up his Blood Pressure to a higher level and will subject his body to boils.
- Blood-related diseases, pain in the spine and heat-prone diseases like smallpox will affect the native.
- The native's father will give more benefits to the native's younger brother.
- The native will not have marital bliss.

Sun + Mercury

- The father of the native will be very brilliant.
- The native may be engaged in small/petty business.
- His younger sister will be very intelligent.
- The native will have mathematical abilities when Mercury is placed next to the Sun and when the Sun is behind Mercury, the native will have less education or engage himself in a job irrelevant to his subject of study.
- It indicates the monetary transactions that prevail between the two and the strength of the business they are engaged in.

Sun + Jupiter

- The native belongs to a highly respectable family, possesses dignity and honesty, spiritually minded.
- He will have abundant income and will be a trustee of a Temple.
- This combination will cause blemish when the authority is abused in the construction of a Common temple or public buildings, using temple funds in unscrupulous ways.
- This purely indicates the existence of the curse of forefathers.

Sun + Venus

- The native's father will be wealthy, and luxurious and will enjoy all the comforts of life but have weak sperm counts.
- He will be fond of his girl children. He will have bright eyes.
- He will spend more on administration and is a spendthrift.

Sun + Saturn

- Enmity between the father and the son will always prevail.
- The father will have a prestigious business which will be passed on to his son who will not inherit his father's properties properly.

- The father will have dark eyes. Female natives will be damsels of their fathers but will not be affectionate towards their mothers.
- Their hereditary business will be as Goldsmiths and the natives will always be interested in it.

Sun + Rahu

- This is termed a Solar Eclipse and indicates that the native's father would have suffered when the native was born.
- There will be a threat to the life of the native's father and problems for his paternal relatives.
- The native will have no or few male children.
- His eyes will be big. The native's father will suffer from heart ailments, pain in the spine, fear of dreams and thunders.
- The income will have a beating.

Sun + Ketu

- The natives will face problems from the Government for misappropriation of Government funds, and punishment by the Government.
- The native's father will have small eyes, and a spiritual nature but will be suffering from small intestine, spinal cord problems, and hip ailments.

Moon + Mars

- The native will have a stout physique and brevity.
- He may suffer blood pressure. Menstruation problems will bother female natives. Blood-related health issues will be there.
- The natives will be engaged in agriculture. The natives will inherit hereditary maternal properties and diseases as well. Siblings will be affectionate with each other.
- The natives will be interested in salty dishes.

Notes:

Among siblings, if one is well off others suffer through many problems. The natives may face danger in water bodies – in watery areas. Most of the queries are directed towards health issues. They are adamant about the construction of a dwelling house. This query should be answered only when the transit Moon passes over this planetary combination.

Moon + Mercury

- This is a strong indicator of the existence of blemish in children termed 'Putradosha'.
- The natives will be strongly imaginative.
- They will have neuro problems (nerve disorders) and mental tension and mental disorders.
- They are dreamers and decisive planners and adhere to their plans.

Moon + Jupiter

- This is considered a good fortune.
- The native will have a round shaped face.
- Sisters born with the native suffer and face hard-core torture.
- The native will deviate and violate a proper life, and suffer scabies and chronic diseases. Blemish through children will prevail.
- The natives will accumulate wealth for their children and will respect and be affectionate towards their mother.

Notes:

This planetary combination represents some objects going missing or stolen. The natives will always be suspicious and suspect the fidelity of their spouse. They will be worried about their ancestral properties. Those who go missing or live in exile, return after a year in a good position and approach astrologers for consultation.

Moon + Venus

- Some notable features are a pretty face, frequent conflict between mother-in-law and daughter-in-law, break or stoppage in education, excessive expenditures, and loss or destruction of possessions and objects.
- There will be a delay in the native's sister getting married.
- Excessive chillness will be the cause of diseases. Loss of wealth and money.
- The presence of Venus will drive the natives to indulge in lustful nature and have extramarital relations.
- Fine Arts, dance and drama, and Literary works are some attires of the natives.

Moon + Saturn (Punarpoo)

- The natives will always be on the move and travel frequently from place to place.
- There will be delays in all the affairs or work undertaken and uncertainty until the completion of the job.
- The natives will suffer calcium deficiency, joint pains and irritation in the foot.
- They will experience late or delayed marriages.
- The natives will easily find fault with others.

Notes:

Astrologers should motivate the natives to patiently wait till the completion of the job as they will succeed after the hurdles. Their success will drive them to thank the astrologers for their encouragement.

Moon + Rahu

- The natives will indulge in a secret marriage and will try to change their religion.
- They will be liars and will get their job done at any cost.

- They will have a bigger left eye. Female natives will suffer from menstruation problems.
- The natives will have a confused mind and be prone to thefts, allergies, insect bites and sweating.
- They are fearful and badly affected.

Moon + Ketu

- The native will have mental stress, strain and Pressure.
- The left eye of the native will be comparatively smaller than his right eye.
- The natives have dejection and a lonely life.
- They will be driven towards suicidal mentalities.
- They will suffer from food poisoning, insect bites, itching, allergies, dry skin, etc.,
- The natives will suffer through family burdens, debt, litigation and life threats
- They will look for legal remedies.
- The mother of the natives will suffer severely.

Mars + Mercury

- The natives will have breaks or interruptions in their studies.
- They will study about machines and possess mathematical research abilities.
- The natives will have a sequence of teeth.
- The natives will possess or inherit buildings and landed properties.
- The natives will be drunkards when these planets align with the Moon.
- Spinsters raise queries about registered marriages or illicit relationship marriages when the transit Moon passes over this planetary alignment.
- Astrologers should exercise caution about marriage-related questions on the day of queries when the transit Moon passes over this planetary combination as this will deceive and distract

the predictions. This planetary combination will cause some turbulence in the minds of women of young age. This will induce temptation to have extramarital or illicit relations like seeking a lover by a married woman or the company of another woman by a married man.

Mars + Jupiter

- The natives will have a strong physique, tamasic nature and fatty body.
- The natives will deal with and swindle others' money.
- They will be affected by blood-related diseases.
- Affliction to this planetary combination will result in chronic diseases like Cancer.
- They will be fond of spicy food.
- The natives will be involved in constructing Temples and Public utility buildings.
- When this planetary combination is afflicted, most natives will be evil persons masquerading as godly.
- The natives will be affectionate towards their siblings.

Mars + Venus

- The natives will have excessive lust and love resulting in the fulfilment of sexual desires.
- The natives may have excessive albumin levels in their bodies and will have thick hair in the chest.
- The natives will have good wives but may get their second child after considerable delay.
- They are designated as 'Jack of all trades' as they know many trades.
- They will own a palatial house.
- This combination of planets extends horrible incidents when afflicted.

Mars + Saturn

- The natives will have combat and fighting nature.
- They will be ferocious, adamant and rebellious.
- Hard workers and will be engaged in machining activities.
- The natives are prone to accidents, and death threats and undergo surgeries.
- Parts of the body that receive the aspect of this planetary combination or in the sign they are associated with will be seriously affected.
- Female natives will have dissatisfaction with their husbands and look to get separated through divorce.
- The natives will be inclined to have old/dilapidated houses.
- This will cause blemish to female natives who will complain about the laziness or inactive/immobile nature of their husbands.
- This planetary combination pushes the natives to muddle their minds about whether to purchase litigated/disputed agricultural lands, old houses, old vehicles, or old types of machinery.

Mars + Rahu

- The natives will face delays or hurdles in their marriages.
- Their landed, house properties will be under litigation or disputes.
- Their neighbours might have married twice or separated after marriage.
- The natives will have dental problems or weak teeth.
- The natives could not extract work from their servants, and harsh behaviour towards them.
- The natives expect 100% perfection in all the jobs and work they are engaged in or from their subordinates and servants.
- The natives will have a tough mind, disrespect towards spouses, formidable character, and blemishes in marriage and acquiring landed properties.

- The natives will suffer a sudden decrease in blood palate count, and anaemia.
- They will acquire buildings that possess Vaastu defects.

Mars + Ketu

- Blemishes in marriage and land-related issues will haunt the natives.
- The natives born under this planetary combination will be engaged in tailoring work, winders, and Carpentry.
- The natives will suffer severe blemishes in marriage forcing them to either remain as bachelors or marry in different castes, communities or religions.
- The natives will worship Kaalbairav.
- The natives will suffer from diseases like ulcers, and pressure.
- Litigation in legally acquired landed properties, houses, and those pledged as securities for land, homes, and vehicle loans.
- Females' who approach astrologers for consultation during the pass over of the transit Moon over this Mars + Ketu planetary combination reveal their miserable lives. This planetary combination affects either their husbands or brothers.

Mercury + Jupiter

- The natives' faces will be round and will be philanthropists and high intellects.
- They will suffer from jaundice.
- The natives will respect elders and reputed persons.

Mercury + Venus

- This fortune is termed 'Madana Gopala Yoga' indirectly referring to the companionship of ladies.
- The natives will be ardent connoisseurs of arts, music lovers, passionate about women and good at seducing females.

- Intellectual lawyers and advocates.
- They will be financiers and extend loans against documents.

Mercury + Saturn

- The natives will either cheat others or will get cheated.
- They will be interested to buy or own vacant lands and will be real estate brokers/sellers
- The native will possess mathematical ability and forge accounts.
- The natives will suffer from windy diseases like Arthritis and rheumatism.
- The natives will have eunuch tendencies and characteristics (hermaphrodites' behaviour).
- They will have good knowledge of maths, and treatises but face nervous disorders.

Mercury + Rahu

- The native will have a big forehead.
- They will pose as highly educated and possess oratory skills.
- The natives will be affected by diseases like itching, skin diseases, allergies, gastric troubles, and black magic and will undergo treatment for the same.
- Maternal uncles of the natives will face problems and be severely affected.

Mercury + Ketu

- The natives behave in a silly manner and have a psychic nature.
- They will possess knowledge of Sastras and scriptures and artistic skills.
- The natives will have delays in their marriages and will be entangled in love affairs.
- Oblivion will be the cause of their failures in education.
- Maternal uncles of the natives will face problems and be severely affected.

Jupiter + Venus

- The placement If this planetary combination is placed in undesired or enemy signs or evolved in the stellium, the natives will face blemishes in their marriages and begetting children.
- Barring Rahu's association (who causes separation or breakups) with this planetary combination, the natives will be engaged in love and love marriages and have good marital bliss.
- The natives will be of fair complexion, and lead a comfortable life but may remain childless or beget children after a long delay.

Notes:

During the transit of the Moon over this planetary combination, natives (with this planetary combination in their natal chart) who are greedy approach the astrologers for consultation but hide their desires.

Jupiter + Saturn

- The natives with such a planetary combination will start working early (even at a tender age).
- They will have bodies of a windy nature and will be prone to neuro problems and suffer from paralysis.
- The natives will be in a good job or profession. Elders in the family may suffer neuro disorders or paralysis.
- Blood relations of the natives may cause problems and shame or dishonour.
- Their devotion will be a big question mark as they choose work as their primary option when asked to choose between God and work.
- During torrid times they will approach God for any relief. Their income will be important and hold a major share in their family but will form part of unquestionable accountability.
- The female siblings will receive wholehearted support from the natives.

- The natives like food especially with a sour taste and their uncontrolled diet habits push them to suffer from all types of diseases.
- Even overnight foods will induce them to eat for days together.
- As they are good earners their management in money matters will be good but they spend big.
- The natives will lead a simple life and succeed.

Jupiter + Rahu

- This refers to the secret defilement of the natives.
- They will distract or disturb Brahmins, Scholars and the learned.
- They will have fatty bodies and be haunted by perennial problems.
- There will be unnatural death in the family and the natives will be stamped as thieves at some point in time.

Jupiter + Ketu

- The natives will have a spiritual nature and saintly thoughts.
- There will be unnatural deaths in the family.
- They will be entangled in huge debt causing unbearable crises.
- At some point, they will be branded as cheats and thieves.
- They will lead a vacuous life.

Venus + Saturn

- The natives will be wealthy but spendthrifts at the same time.
- They will get a good business income.
- Females in the natives' families will make their living/earnings.
- Old friendships will resurface again someday for sure.

Venus + Rahu

- The natives will face all types of women-related problems.
- The natives will face blemishes in having multiple wives and unbearable pain and problems through them to the extent of getting divorced from them.

- The natives' wives will be prone to accidents, misfortunes, near-death consequences, chronic diseases and acquire bad names in society.
- The attitude and deeds of the big-mouthed wives will cause mental stress to the natives.
- Some of the Women having such planetary combinations in their natal (birth) charts will be influenced by misconduct and bad characters pushing them into having illegal/illicit relationships for gains in media, cinema and in the field of arts.
- Most of the females who make pleasant love will cause problems once they get married.
- Monetary transactions by anyone of any type with women who have this planetary combination in their natal chart will lead to litigation at some point in time facing criminal punishment.
- Though such a planetary combination causes an economic crisis, it will extend unexpected fortunes through monetary gains.

Venus + Ketu

- The natives suffer all types of problems like separation of wives from life, harassment of wives with the support of Police and Legal actions, and unrespectful attitudes.
- Dowry harassment cases filed by such women leading towards divorce may bring a bad name to the natives.
- Electronic gadgets play havoc and a vital role in rattling the lives of the natives.

Saturn + Rahu

- Persons with this type of planetary combination will be labourers or coolies/servants and face immense crises in their jobs/work.
- They will be afflicted by Blackmagic or voodoo.
- They may strike/quit their job suddenly.
- They will change their lifestyle suddenly and suffer due to it.
- Even persons of repute slide downwards.

- This will induce the natives to engage in unlawful activities.
- The natives will always face economic struggles or against their relatives.
- The natives will own an independent nature and keep causing disputes and disturbances in the family. They will either follow modern culture or stick to age-old practices causing havoc in others' lives through their wretched behaviour.

Saturn + Ketu

- The natives will be inclined towards spiritualism.
- They will be machine operators and handle machines.
- They will face hardships in their business and face betrayal by business partners.
- The natives could not find relations suitable to their tastes and expectations in their lives.
- But this combination will not hinder those who lead a calm life without any great desires or expectations.

Rahu + Ketu

- This combination occurs when these two nodes cross over each other's degree positions in transit.
- This transit completely shifts the path of life and trembles the very basic life structure of the natives.
- The nodes cause blemishes through their association with any planet.
- Many unnatural deaths, accidents and cruel ends.
- This transitory combination unroots many Dynasties and annihilates them.

Manthi

Manthi is identified as a sub-lord and depicted as the son of Saturn in the epics. Manthi's position is marked in the Zodiac and also in Prasanna as an important significator of malefic influences.

Manthi calculations

For Manthi calculations, we need to know

1. The Sun's position in degrees should be reckoned
2. Whether the Computation of Manthi is for Daytime or nighttime

Add weekdays Manthi degree to Sun's position to know Manthi's position

Sl No.	Weekday	Degrees are to be added for	
		Day	Night
1.	Sunday	156	240
2.	Monday	132	216
3.	Tuesday	108	192
4.	Wednesday	84	336
5.	Thursday	60	312
6.	Friday	36	288
7.	Saturday	12	264

To remember the daytime Manthi position in degrees easily, a day consists of 24 hours

To know each day's Manthi position during day time:

Saturday's position is 12 degrees and by adding 24 degrees to this, 36 degrees is Friday Manthi's position

Friday's Manthi position is 36 degrees and by adding 24 degrees to this, 60 degrees is Thurs day's Manthi position

Thursday's Manthi position is 60 degrees and by adding 24 degrees to this, 84 degrees is Wednesday's Manthi position

Wednesday's Manthi position is 84 degrees and by adding 24 degrees to this, 108 degrees is Tuesday's Manthi position

Tuesday's Manthi position is 108 degrees and by adding 24 degrees to this, 132 degrees is Monday's Manthi position

Monday's Manthi position is 132 degrees and by adding 24 degrees to this, 156 degrees is Sunday's Manthi position

Days are in descending order and positional degrees 24 are added every day. We need to remember Saturday as the beginning day and its position is 12 degrees.

To remember the time Manthi position easily, a day consists of 24 hours

To know each day's Manthi during the Night time:

Tuesday's Manthi position is 192 degrees and by adding 24 degrees to this, 216 degrees is Monday's Manthi position during Night

Monday's Manthi position is 216 degrees and by adding 24 degrees to this, 240 degrees is Sunday's Manthi position during Night

Sunday's Manthi position is 240 degrees and by adding 24 degrees to this, 264 degrees is Saturday's Manthi position during Night

Saturday's Manthi position is 264 degrees and by adding 24 degrees to this, 288 degrees is Friday's Manthi position during Night

Friday's Manthi position is 288 degrees and by adding 24 degrees to this, 312 degrees is Thursday's Manthi position during Night

Thursday's Manthi position is 312 degrees and by adding 24 degrees to this, 336 degrees is Wednesday's Manthi position during Night

Weekdays are in descending order and position gets added by 24 degrees for each day. Just we need to remember that, Tuesday is the starting day at 192 degrees.

Getting to know the Daytime Manthi on a Thursday, September 1971

Sun's position	-	145 degrees

Thursday, daytime Manthi position	-	60 degrees
Manthi's position from Sun	-	145 + 60 = 205 degrees

205 degrees denotes Star Visaka Part 2 in Libra Sign @ Thula Rasi

Thursday Night time Manthi position

Sun's position	-	145 degrees
Thursday-Night time Manthi position	-	312 degrees
Manthi's position from Sun	-	145 + 312 = 457 degrees

457 degrees more than 360 degrees, 457-360 = 97 degrees 97/30 = 3 signs = 7degress in fourth. It indicates Cancer Sign @ Kataka Rasi Star Poosam (Pushya) part 2.

Manthi indicates severe blemish. In conjunction with Rahu and Ketu, the severity is manyfold.

Manthi's conjunction with Planets denotes the blemish relates to that Planet's Kargathuva @ characteristics.

Effects of Manthi with Other Planets

Sun + Manthi

Implies lethality to paternal side, blemishes, and curses present. It indicates the blemish descended from ancestral genre and prevention from enjoying the benefits from ancestral properties. It brings disgrace in own community/group.

Moon + Manthi

Indicates lethality on the maternal side, blemishes, and curses present. It implies the blemish descended from the mother's side genre and separation amongst the relations, mental fears, and sudden mental aberrations.

Mars + Manthi

Blood-related lethal implications, blemishes, blemish impact on siblings, and curses present. It causes diseases and enmity.

Mercury + Manthi

Lethal implications to maternal uncles, blemishes, and curses are shown by this combination. The native will be impacted by the curses/ blemishes of spinsters/unmarried women and will lack grasping.

Jupiter + Manthi

Genetic lethality, blemishes, and progenitor curses are indicated by this combination. This will affect the children.

The native will not get a good preceptor and will not beget the desired children. Even when desired children are born, they will choose their life path.

Venus + Manthi

Blemishes through women, curses of women, women inherited blemishes will haunt the natives. It shows the blemish and lethality through the wife.

Saturn + Manthi

It indicates the strong curse/blemish of family/tutelary deities. It strongly indicates unfulfilled offerings/submissions to family/tutelary deities. The native will not have good servants/sub-ordinates/employees and will not get any job/income that is worth his knowledge/education/ capabilities. This placement causes separation within relations and mental and startling fear.

Rahu + Manthi

Lethality, blemishes, and curses drawn from forefathers of the paternal side are indicated. The native will fear poisoning/intoxication. Disgrace, humiliation, and loss will chase the natives. Big mortality will horrify the natives.

Ketu + Manthi

Lethality, blemishes, and curses drawn from forefathers of the maternal side are indicated. The native will fear poisoning/intoxication. Disgrace, humiliation, and loss will chase the natives. The native will face separation and legal cases and will receive punishment.

Ascendant + Manthi

There will be life threats to the natives and lethal situations will appear before sight.

Whichever planet travels over Manthi, leads to death.

The transit Moon over natal (birth) Manthi exposes the mental status of the native and the incidents that have happened or are about to happen. The native for whom the transit Moon is passing over the natal (birth) Manthi hears about the death of a person.

Manthi's Presence in All the 12 Bhavas or Houses

Manthi in the ascendant

There will be a flash or bright difference from others. Longevity will be there. Good wealth or properties, stealing habits, blockhead or stupid, will have no descendants, will have no inclinations to common things, seething rage.

Manthi in the 2nd house to the ascendant

Will indulge in in-clashes, will not keep his word, will create confusion amongst family members through his word, is spendthrift, and will have eye defects.

Manthi in the 3rd house to the ascendant

He will always be fighting with his elder siblings, rough courage, self-relapse, egoism, self-prestige, haughtiness, and unknown sorrow.

Manthi in 4th house to ascendant

May separate from family, will have no affection will have vehicles.

Manthi in 5th house to ascendant

Will win over enemies, have malignant influence in having children, will not hop over hereditary practices, devotion towards communal deities, will have disturbed mind and will do menial jobs.

Manthi in the 6th house to the ascendant

Will have a helping tendency, hard worker, will conquer his enemies, will be kind and affectionate with others, habituated to occult sciences.

Manthi in the 7th house to the ascendant

Spouses will be subject to life threats, loss and shame due to cases, dejection in life, the occurrence of debt-related problems, relapses despite hard work, and will be fond of bad women, and thankless people.

Manthi in 8th house to ascendant

Life threat in water, life threat due to liquor consumption, finding fault with others, facial diseases, facial aberration, always prone to problems, dwarf appearance.

Manthi in 9th house to ascendant

Will have hereditary malignant influences, threat of life to father, will spend hard-earned money in faulty ways for bad things and acts.

Manthi in 10th house to ascendant

Will be a niggard, will not donate with a free mind, will eye others' property, friends and relatives will part ways, will have no self-respect.

Manthi in 11th house to ascendant

Will have profitability, will have fame and good physique, will be funny and be always humorous. He will be in interested practising magic.

Manthi in 12th house to ascendant

Will spend family properties, will be good at pawning or pledging properties, spendthrift. If a business or work is pre-closed, Manthi and

Moon will be responsible in their zodiac chart. Will also lose money in alchemy and treasure hunt.

Manthi's conjunction with any Planet will indicate blemish or malediction only.

The aspect of Jupiter will reduce the malignant influence. Manthi's conjunction with Badagathipathi or malefic distress causing Planets, will frighten the querist first and then will punish him.

Manthi's conjunction with Planets of the 8th house

Malignant influences will frighten the querist and will then leave away. If the 8th house Lord, malefic Planets and Manthi conjoin together, malignant influence will frighten the querist and his family and then punish them. The punishment will be very cruel.

Manthi's conjunction with Trine Lords

It indicates that the malignant influences continue and have hereditary influence.

Diamond and Yellow Topaz reduces Manthi's malignant influences

Mantras chanted for Planet Saturn reduce Manthi's blemish. Sudarshana Homa reduces the malignant influences of Manthi. Unani and ayurvedic medical treatment are the best ways to treat diseases influenced by Manthi. Only a doctor specialised in Siddha medicine can treat and cure diseases caused by Manthi.

Karakathuva @ Accomplishment of Planets

A planet may have one life and one lifeless object for its accomplishment @ Karaguthuva in astrology. We should learn both and put them to appropriate use. By gaining knowledge about planetary accomplishments or Planets associated with their instrumental deeds, their character, and relativity theory, an astrologer can raise his image. Let us know some more about Planets.

Sun

The Sun is considered to be tall, fiery in nature, dark brown colour, scanty hair, bald head, bilious nature, indicator of father, vitality, masculine, malefic, copper colour, ego, Royal, philosophical tendency, money lenders, will power, authority and position. He rules fuel, hides and skin, wool, weapons, silk cloth, pungent flavour, husk of grains, wheat, gold, fire, medicines, doctors, Kings and Statesmen. Sun is the producer and developer of seeds. He is the soul of the Universe, the power to resist diseases, pearl, wood, lion, strength, worship of Lord Shiva, thorny trees, the benevolence of King (Now Government), Magistrate, gold ornaments, physician, electric current, ambassador and ophthalmology.

Also, he is responsible for Soul, banishment, Sea voyage, Integrity, Hope belief, relationships and personality.

Places

Open places, range of mountains and hills, forests, Capital towns and places of worship. Shiva temple, Ocean, Courts, exhibitions, social gatherings, fort, a region where there is no water and eastern side quarter.

Parts of Body

Sun controls the head, stomach, bones, heart, arteries (blood circulation), eyes, brain, throat, spleen, belly and strength of tissues.

Diseases

Diseases caused by the Sun are high blood pressure, high fever, cerebral disorders, eye diseases, throat, ear and nose diseases, consumption and dysentery. When Sun in watery signs afflicted by malefic Planets in unfavourable houses water-prone diseases are indicated.

Sun indicates Kshatriya Caste and his Sex is male.

God

Sun indicates worship of Light, Lord Shiva and Gods without a proper structure.

Moon

Moon defines a fat body, young as well as old, white in complexion, curly hair, and lovely eyes. She is the ruler of mind and intelligence, mental disposition, heart, mother, beauty, a saturation of blood, renowned persons, young women, people who are interested in walking, soft in speech, magnetic force, scent, juice, fickle-minded and very lustful. Watery substances, lakes, Sea, temple of Goddess Durga, vegetation, rain, textile, fine chemicals and pharmaceuticals, alcohol, milk, honey, sugarcane, pearls, sweet things, rice, barley, wheat and agriculturists.

Parts of the Body

Arteries, nerves, brain, fat, stomach, Uterus, bladder, breast, ovaries and organs of procreation are ruled by the Moon.

Diseases

Diseases caused by Moon are venereal diseases, jaundice, dyspepsia, asthma, bronchitis, skin diseases etc., She is phlegmatic and windy.

Moon represents Vaishya Caste and feminine gender and has Northwest as her direction.

Mars

Mars denotes slender waist, curly and shining hair, fierce red eye, cruel nature and fickle mind. Mars is a naturally malefic Planet. He represents younger brother, masculine, blood-red colour, refined taste base, rotten things, ambassadors, military activities, commerce, aerial journeys, weaving public speakers. Mars denotes red colour, hot and fiery, limbs, Urinary system, logic, fireplaces, kitchen, engine room, boiler, night workers, murders, conspiracy, strikes, enemy, wounds, organising capacity, executive abilities, leadership over labourers, police department and scandals.

Materials governed by Mars are copper, metals, mines, minerals and ores, gold fields, coral, weapons, land and tobacco.

Parts of Body

Parts of the body ruled by Mars are bile, ears, nose, forehead, sinews, fibre and muscular tissues

Diseases Caused by Mars

Rupture of Veins and arteries, diseases of bone marrow, haemorrhage, abortions, menstrual disorders, gonorrhoea, muscular rheumatism, humps and burns.

Mars represents the Kshatriya Caste and Masculine in Gender.

His direction is South.

Mercury

Mercury is benefic when associated with benefic Planets and becomes malefic when associated with malefic Planets.

Mercury is knitted with fun. Mercury represents intelligence and is known to possess a lot of information. Mercury is called the prince of heavenly bodies. Earthy in Composition, spare, thin and green in colour, mercantile activity, public speaking, cold and nervous. He rules over Commerce, Churches, Schools, Playgrounds, Parks, gambling dens and delights in damage.

Mercury governs emerald, lead, oilseeds, green gram, edible oils, currency, alloys and brass.

Other things ruled by Mercury are mechanics, clerks, water, poetry intellect, education, authorships, maternal uncles, maternal grandfathers and paternal relatives, palatial buildings, horses, doctors and traders.

Parts of Body

The brain, tongue, nervous system, thyroid glands, skin, neck and power of speech are governed by Mercury

Diseases

Dumbness, insanity, loss of memory, headache and skin diseases, fits, smallpox, plenty of bile, phlegm and wind in composition.

Mercury represents Vaishya Caste and Eunuch in Sex. Mercury rules over the North direction.

Jupiter

Those born under Jupiter's influence will have brown eyes and brown hair, tall body, fat and phlegmatic with a tall and heavy carrier, corpulence, loud and heavy voice, Masculine, benefic, bright yellow colour, devotion, progeny, truthfulness, religious fervour, philosophical and aptitude for every science.

It represents wealth, fame, sons and grandsons, children, learned men, grandfather, intellect, education, Minister, advisor, ether, scriptures, quicksilver, cardamoms, banks and insurance companies.

Jupiter is the essence of knowledge and wisdom, the preceptor of God. He represents topaz, treasure houses and places where learned men live. Gold is the metal wealth.

Parts of Body

He has domain over fat, stomach and intestine in the body.

Diseases

The diseases caused by him are liver troubles, dropsy, flatulence, abscess, carbuncles, degeneration of fat, digestive troubles and kidney-related related.

Jupiter is also known as Deva Guru and Gnana Karaka.

He belongs to the Brahmin Caste and Male gender.

His direction is Northeast.

Venus

Venus indicates black curly hair, huge body, wheaty complexion, a feminine, benefic, mixture of all colours, wife, love affairs, sensual pleasures, family bliss, vitality, watery in composition with white body and charming appearance, spouse, dance halls, sexual happiness etc.,

Venus rules over vehicles, sugar cane industries, trade chemicals, medicine, silk, fine quality cotton, luxury articles, passion, pleasure, maidservants, perfumes and musical instruments.

Parts of Body

Sexual organs and semen, muscles, thighs, Urine and hair are ruled by Venus.

Diseases

Venus causes diseases like venereal complaints, sexual disability, muscular rheumatism, loss of eyesight and power of smell, spermatorrhoea and leucorrhoea.

Venus indicates the Brahmin Caste and female gender.

She owns Southeast Direction.

Saturn

Our Sages considered Saturn as the major Planet revolving around Outer Orbit and is farthest from the Sun placing it along Jupiter and Mars.

Saturn-influenced persons will have stiff hair, large limbs, dark bodies, malefic, stubbornness, impetuosity, demoralisation, windy diseases, despondency, and gambling tendencies. He rules the Air, mountains and hills, forest regions and dirty places. He has domain over iron, sapphire, cremation grounds and burial places, prisons and old people. The commodities presided over by him are black gram, hemp, barley and oils.

Parts of Body

Saturn rules over bladder, excretory system, teeth, muscles, wrist and feet.

Disease

Diseases caused by Saturn are muscular pains, toothache, asthma, tuberculosis, epilepsy, hysteria, pains in the joints and ulcers.

Saturn belongs to the Shudra Caste and Eunuch in gender. It controls the West direction.

Rahu

Malefic, feminine, renunciation, corruption, epidemics, tall and phlegmatic, dark in complexion and dirty are the Characteristics of Rahu. Rahu is materialistic, induces foreign travels and intrigues low-class people. Also, it indicates paternal grandfather and maternal grandmother.

Parts of Body

The parts of the body ruled by Rahu are skin and blood.

Diseases

Diseases caused by Rahu are Cholera, smallpox, leprosy, epilepsy, blood poisoning, itches, malaria and plague.

It belongs to the low Caste and Eunuch in Gender. It controls the Southwest Direction.

Ketu

Ketu is dark in complexion, smoky colour, tall and inhaling smoke. It rules maternal grandfather and paternal grandmother. Malefic, religious, sectarian principles, pride, selfishness, and occultism are its characteristics

Diseases

Ketu indicates intestinal worms, smallpox, cholera and other epidemics. He generally causes the same diseases as Rahu.

Ketu represents Low Caste and Hermaphrodite in Sex. And has Southwest as the direction.

Given above are the Characteristics of 9 Planets Sun, Moon, Mars, Mercury, Jupiter, Venus, Saturn, Rahu and Ketu. Karakathuvas @ Characteristics of these nine Planets have to be memorized. To predict a horoscope or Prasanna, this is very essential to say what kind of job or business the native will do, and whether a particular incident will happen or not. In the case of a student, he can be guided to decide his future course/branch of study. Each Planet indicates its respective action-oriented objectives.

Notes:

Sun is depicted as Pitru Karaka as we know about one's father and father-related work through him.

Moon is Mathur Karaka and all about a mother and her ancestors can be known.

Mars is Bratru Karaka and also Boomi Karaka who tells about siblings and land belongings.

Mercury is Vidya Karaka to say about Education.

Jupiter is Dhana Karaka to talk about one's wealth and children.

Venus is known as the Kalatra Karaka which helps to know about one's spouse and the sensual and sexual pleasures one can have.

Saturn or Ayul Karaka denote the longevity of a Native.

Rahu as Gnana Karaka helps One to get Wisdom.

Ketu as Motcha Karaka helps to get eternal bliss.

Apart from the Nine Planets, one more celestial body known as Manthi or Kuligan can be seen in Zodiac squares. Manthi is none other than Saturn's son.

ன

Karakathuvas of Bhava or Houses

Karakathuva of 1st Bhava @ House

The 1st square of the ascendant is called the 1st bhava or house. It indicates permanent relationship links like Father, Mother, Native, and Caste etc., Through this a Querist's (Querist is the one who puts the question to know his future and fortune or asks some questions to know the answers) life, body, head, character, colour, appearance, capacity, inheritance of other's money etc., can be known.

In parts of the body, it denotes the head.

Karakathuvas of 2nd Bhava or House

This represents the family, word wealth and vaksthana (speech) of the querist. Through this querist's well-being, wealth, education, eloquence, food, right eye, face, family, scientific wisdom, teeth new members to the family, the addition of new things, gold ornaments, and unexpected gains can be known.

In parts of the body, it denotes the face.

Karakathuvas of 3rd Bhava or House

Known as the Brathrusthana of the querist, this is an indicator of siblings. The third house rules courage, vitality, evil inclinations, short journeys, brother and sisters, right ear and help. Also, it denotes expenditure, information, property sales, medical expenses relating to mother, kindness, musical prowess, ancestral debts, religious differences and dreams.

In parts of the body, it denotes the neck.

Karakathuvas of 4th Bhava or House

This is referred to as Sukasthana @ zone of comfort. Also, it is known as matrusthana and vakanasthana (Transport) of the querist which means this house indicates about his mother, comforts and vehicles owned. Through this, the physical well-being of the mother, domestic bliss of the querist, vehicle possession, house and landed property, education level, possession of domestic animals like cow, goat, sheep, relatives and friends, primary education, sorrow, treasure, lakes, well, greeneries or groves, matter relating to son-in-law or daughter-in-law can be known.

In parts of the body, it denotes the heart.

Karakathuvas of the 5th Bhava or House

5th House of Bhava is known as Puthrasthana indicator of children along with past noble deeds, place of fortune, fame and prosperity. Also, whether the querist is an Atheist or believer of Theism can be known.

The grace of children, great grandfather, fortunes, tantric bliss, maternal uncle, stomach disorders, mind, desires, knowledge, wisdom, future, prosperity, yoga practice, profits through race and lottery, presenting deity, blessings of deity, tutelary deity's stature, books, fiction writing abilities, chanting of Vedas, intelligence etc., are indicated by this bhava or house.

It denotes the abdomen or stomach part of the body.

Karakathuvas of the 6th Bhava or House

6th House is known as Shatrusthana or about enemies. It defines enemies, debt and diseases. Sixth Bhava or House denotes the querist's enemies, bad happenings, diseases he is likely affected with, his debts, court cases, oblivion or forgetfulness, hunger, thirst, accidents, jail, criminal offences, prone to theft, labour work, shocking incidents.

It signifies the abdomen or stomach part of the body.

Karakathuvas of 7th Bhava or House

This is called the Kalasthrasthana @ house indicating life partner.

Indications about life partners, and sexual pleasures are through this Bhava or House.

Through this, lust, fondness, the portion below the umbilical cord, partnership, about wife if a male and about husband, if the querist is a female, marriage, ups and downs of family life, pilgrimage, and business partner, can be seen as seventh place indicators.

It denotes the middle part of the body.

Karakathuvas of 8th Bhava or House.

8th house is known as Ayursthana @ about longevity

Through this Bhava, a querist can know about his longevity, disgrace he may be facing, deriving unexpected money, lottery, treasure, dangers, evil repute, cause and place of death, servants, chronic diseases and obstructions, dowry, slavery and jail, sorrows of debt, loneliness, divorce and laziness.

The 8th house also denotes the mangalyasthana of a married woman. Torture, unnatural death in female horoscopes, eloping or running away secretly, extramarital affairs, demands etc., can be seen.

It denotes Genitals among parts of the body.

Karakathuvas of 9th Bhava or House

9th House or Bhava is known as the Pithrusthana indicator of the father and his status.

Through this, the paternal side of the querist, fortune, ancestral properties, yoga or home offerings to the fire god, construction of temples, caste, community, religion, sea voyage, scientific wisdom, long journeys, pilgrimage, possession of the horse, elephant, milking herds like a cow, sheep, Teacher, temple renovation, attainment of Eight supernatural powers by yoga are all indicated.

9th House or Bhava indicates Thigh's part of the body.

Karakathuvas of the 10th Bhava or House

It is also known as Jivanasthana @ Survival

This House indicates the Karma and work of a querist in astrology and Prasanna. Through this, a querist's job or work, power, fortunes, yaga @ offerings to God through fire, food taste, nullifying father's karmic deeds, occult sciences, governance, and Government job can be known.

In parts of the body, it represents the knees.

Karakathuvas of 11th Bhava or House

11th Bhava or House is defined as Labasthana @ profit or fortune

Known for querist's desires, profitability, and elder siblings. Through this the querist can know his profitability through business or work and other income, about elder siblings, left ear, ankles, attainment of wealth, profits through communication, sea voyage, etc.,

In parts of the body, it denotes ankles.

Karakathuvas of 12th Bhava or House

12th Bhava or House is called the Mokshasthana @ attainment of Mukti

It is an indicator of wasteful expenditure, losses, food, sleep, sexual pleasures, left eye, rebirth, salvation, suicidal death, treason, caste conversion, foreign domicile, jail, hospital stay, peaceful mind, no peace of mind, silence, loneliness, foreign travel, living in another state, unknown places, medical labs.

In parts of the body, it denotes the Foot.

All the above Karakathuvas are the subject matter of Planets posited in these Bhavas or Houses, Planets in conjunction and aspect these houses

Karakathuvas of Rasis @ Signs

Aries @ Mesham

It is movable, odd, masculine, cruel, fiery, of short ascension, rising by hinder part @ Prishtodaya

Aries also denotes a place of jewels metals, fire, the earth's surface, having jewels and minerals underneath, Travelling during daytime in forests and nighttime in cities or villages, blood-red in colour, lunar sign, malefic, strong, abodes in the forest. Aries born will have round eyes, square faces, good practicability, social, bad temper, and does not hesitate in utter falsehood. Rajoguna predominates and is blind in the dead of night.

Taurus @ Rishabam

It is Fixed, even, feminine, mild, earthly, fruitful, of short ascension, rising by hinder part @ Prishtodaya.

Taurus also indicates the forest or field land where cattle or agriculturists reside, a field with water where paddy is grown, white in colour, lunar sign, benefic, broad thighs big face, forgiving, hardship, prominent eyes, behave like a bull, practicability, bad temper when provoked, villages, businessmen and strong at night.

Gemini @ Mithunam

It is common, odd, masculine, cruel, airy, barren, of short ascension, rising by the head @ Shirsodaya. Gemini indicates places where dancers, singers, artists, and women of pleasure reside, a bedroom, the place for sexual enjoyment and indoor sports, places where cards or other kinds of betting going on, and gambling dens etc., It has a parrot-green colour, lunar sign, average ascension, curly hair, skilled in interpreting other people's thoughts, an elevated nose, likes music and housekeeping, slender arms and long fingers, lives in villages and blind at midday.

Cancer @ Katakam

Even, Movable, feminine, mild, watery, of long ascension, fruitful and rising by hinder part @ Prishtodaya.

Cancer also describes watery fields where paddy is grown, wells and tanks, river banks where there are abundant plants shrubs and trees due to moisture and extra humidity, a chasm with water, whitish-red colour, lunar sector, fast in walking, fond of wealth, occult tendencies, benefic sign, saturated disposition, social nature, not selfish but sacrifices for others.

Leo @ Simmam

Fixed, odd, masculine, cruel, fiery, medium ascension, barren, rising by the head @ Shirsodaya

The regions of the deep forest, mountains, hills and hillocks, forts, pale-white like smoke colour, solar sign, spine part of the body, abode in caves and mountains etc., reddish eyes, large cheeks, broad face, honourable, malefic sign, blind at dead night are the significance of Leo sign.

Virgo @ Kanni

Common, even, feminine, mild, earthy, of long ascension, rising by the head @ shirsodaya

The place of artisanship, place of enjoyment of women, pasture land, land with water, land with corn, multicoloured (colour-variegated), benefic, medium ascension, vegetation land, shoulders and arms dropping, truthful and kindly, limited number of issues, dark hair, good mental ability, methodical and critical, solar sign, blind at midday are the indicators of Virgo Sign.

Libra @ Thulam

Movable, odd, masculine, cruel, airy, of long ascension, rising by the head @ Shirsodaya

High land where corn is grown (grain is the chief commodity or merchandize and libra represents weighing scale), place of businesses or offices, street shops, a rich man's place of abode, a merchant's house, black colour, solar sign, medium ascension, market place, fair appearance, impartial in argument, brave, slender body in youth but bends to corpulence (hefty or fat), round face, good complexion, malefic are the significance of Libra Sign

Libra represents the Kidney and uterus in the parts of the body.

Scorpio @ Vrichigam

Fixed, even, feminine, mild, watery, of long ascension, rising by the head @ Shirsodaya

Scorpio signifies places having holes or cavities where serpents (snakes) and others live, poison, crevices in hillocks or mountains, hidden places, caves, golden colour, solar sign, benefic, secret part of the human body, long ascension, broad eyes and a broad chest, suffer from diseases in early age, will do cruel acts, self-reliance, courage, endurance and executive ability.

Sagittarius @ Danus

Common, odd, masculine, cruel, fiery, of long ascension, rising by hinder part @ Prishtodaya

The places where authorities live or work, horses, chariots and elephants live, the King's residence etc., are represented by Sagittarius. Brownish colour, solar sign, malefic, abodes battlefield, long face and neck, big ears and nose, great strength, liberal, cheerful, noble at heart, like physical culture and travelling and having loud voice are other significators of Sagittarius.

Capricorn @ Makaram

Movable, even, feminine, mild, earthy, of long ascension, rising by hinder part @ Prishtodaya

Rivers, forests, watery places, rich or abundance of water, banks or sides of rivers or mountains, wheating yellow colour, solar sign, benefic, average ascension, weak in the lower limbs, good strength, indolent, prominent nose etc., are the significators of Capricorn sign.

Aquarius @ Kumbam

Fixed, odd, masculine, cruel, fruitful, airy, short ascension, rising by the head @ Shirsodaya

Places, where water has dried up, where men who manufacture liquors or birds live, places in the house where pots are kept, the place frequented by potters, darkish-white in colour, lunar sign, legs, malefic, strong in day, fair looking, intellectual, dark hair and has the forgiving temperament, are some of the significations of Aquarius sign.

Pisces @ Meenam

Common, feminine, watery, even mild, of short ascension, rising by the head and hinder part @ Ubhayodaya sign.

Pisces signifies religious and holy places, rivers where sacred baths are undertaken, seas, oceans, places where there are temples and shrines, violet colour, lunar sign, benefic, symmetrical and shining body, fond of wife, learned and reserved etc., It represents Foot in the body part.

Graha Kochara @ Planetary Movements in Zodiac

Time taken by each planet to move through each sign of the Zodiac:

Sun travels roughly One degree in a day, 30 days to cross one sign and 365.6 days to complete a round of the Zodiac.

Moon travels one degree in One hour 48 minutes and takes 2-1/4 (two and a quarter days) to pass through each sign and in all takes roughly 27 days to complete a round of the Zodiac.

Mars takes 1-1/2 days to cross one degree and takes 45 days to complete a round of a Zodiac

Mercury travels 1-1/2 degrees in a day. (i.e., within 28 degrees from the Sun) and roughly takes a month to pass over each sign.

Venus takes one day to pass over a degree and in approximately 30 days it crosses a sign.

Jupiter takes one year to pass through one sign but for a complete round of Zodiac, it takes l   little less than 12 years.

Saturn takes 2-1/2 years to pass through One sign.

Rahu takes 18 months to travel One sign.

Ketu takes 18 months to travel One sign.

Here Saturn takes the longest period to pass over a sign while Moon takes the shortest time of 2-1/4 days to cross a sign.

Transformation of Natal Planets during Transit

The planetary strength should be ascertained depending on their natal positions and during transit.

While the strength of Exalted Venus posited in Pisces in the natal (birth) chart gets 100% strength it gains only 50% strength when positioned in Taurus during transit though it rules Taurus. This reduces its natural Karaka characteristics but extends its bhava results in full.

Assuming the same Venus in its debilitation position in Virgo while in exaltation position in the natal (birth) chart, the strength gets further reduced to only 25%.

The application and assessment of the strength are on similar lines when a planet is associated/conjoined with a planet in a sign depending on their interrelationship as friendlier, neutral or inimical nature. The results should be declared accordingly.

This can be compared to a person's character change and growth from childhood to adulthood as years pass by.

It is my strong conclusion based on my research that during transit planets increase or decrease the strength of natal planets.

Transit Rules

Explanation 1

Inimical Planetary alignments in a birth chart, when positioned in the same inimical alignments in Transit, give more vulnerability. As already they have with inimical attitude in the birth chart, alignment in Transit makes them more vulnerable giving more impact.

Explanation 2

Inimical Planetary alignments in a birth chart, when associated with its friendly planet in Transit, limit its inimical quality. An inimical Planet's qualities subsidize, as association with a friendly Planet reduces the temperament.

Explanation 3

A native will bear the inimical impact if the Maha Dasha (Dasha), Antar Dasha (Bukthi), and Prityandar Dasha (Antaram) are favourable to him even though the current Transit of Planets are against him. On the contrary, he suffers heavily if the current Maha Dasha (Dasha), Antar Dasha (Bukthi), and Prityandar Dasha (Antaram) are unfavourable and the Transit is also vulnerable.

Explanation 4

A Planet associated with several Planets in a house of a birth chart exhibits characteristics of those planets during the Transit period. A lone Planet alone exhibits its characteristics during Transit.

Explanation 5

A Planet posited in a particular degree of a Sign/Rasi will extend the benefits or Karaka of some other Planets posited in the same degree in any Sign/Rasi, during its Transit, Dasha period.

Explanation 6

During the transit into a Sign/Rasi, if a planet does not find any other Planet in that Sign/Rasi, then the Planet does not have any materialistic impact on the life of the Native.

It is something like finding the house locked when visiting a Guest.

Explanation 7

During the transit into a Sign/Rasi, if a planet finds its friendly Planet in that Sign/Rasi, then the Planet will extend good benefits to the native.

It resembles finding some lovable person in a house while visiting a house.

Explanation 8

During the transit into a Sign/Rasi, if a planet finds its inimical Planet in that Sign/Rasi, then the Planet will extend evil benefits to the native.

Explanation 9

During the transit into a Sign/Rasi, if a planet finds more than one Planet in that Sign/Rasi, then the Planet should give the benefits of all the planets posited. It extends the benefits based on the degree of the position of other Planets from it.

For example,

If Saturn enters Leo Sign where two of its inimical Planets and one of its friendly Planet are posited, then Saturn has to extend two portions of malefic results and one portion of benefic result to the native. Saturn will extend malefic results till it crosses the inimical Planets and benefic results while crossing the benefic Planet.

Ohm Sree Uchista Maha Ganapathaye Namah:

CHANDRA NAADI

A Recap of Rules and its Application

Essential factors:

1. Karakathuvas @ accomplishments of the planets.
2. Results of planetary combinations/conjunctions.
3. Planetary Aspects.
4. Karakathuvas @ accomplishments of the Signs/Rasi, Bhavaga positions.
5. Degree-wise Transit positions (Gochara) of the planets at the time and day of consultation.
6. A clear and distinct knowledge of the above facilitates the declaration of 80% results using 'Chandra Naadi' at ease. The Karakathuva of the Star-Lord of the transit day in question activates/accelerates the thoughts and deeds in the mind of the querist. The position of the transit Moon in the sign of the natal (birth) chart of the querist portrays the question and answer that may evolve in the mind of the querist.

There are only **Four** fundamental rules that govern 'Chandra Naadi'. The natal (birth) chart of the native (the person to whom the question relates) and the transit chart showing the planetary positions of the day of the query are essential.

Rule No. 1:

Consider the natal (birth) chart planet/s posited or aspect the Sign/Rasi in which the transit Moon is traversing/passing. Those planets are responsible for the questions in the mind of the querist and answer to the same.

(In other words, ascertain the position of the transit Moon in the Sign/Rasi under the influence of the natal (birth) chart planets by their presence alone or conjoined with other planets or through their aspect of that Sign/Rasi)

Rule No 2: (Past)

Things of the past enjoyed/experienced (good or bad) can be ascertained depending on the passing by/crossing over the natal (birth) chart planet posited in the previous Sign/Rasi by the transit Moon.

Rule No 3: (Present)

Depending upon the natal (birth) chart planet/s posited in the Sign/Rasi which the transit Moon is about to touch and move over will be the present position of the querist.

Rule No 4: (Future)

It depends upon the traverse of the transit Moon to the next Sign/Rasi. The results can be based on two methods: by computing the time of natal Jupiter's aspect on the transit Moon and by the movement of the transit Moon touching the Karakathuva of the query.

Exceptional Rule:

The transit Moon traversing in the 6th, 8th or 12th position to any of the natal (birth) chart planets will indicate life threats, turmoil and serious troubles to its Karakathuvas or Karakathuva relations and will not promise any development.

'Chandra Naadi' – Application through an example

1. Check for the position of the transit Moon on the date and time of query.
2. E.g. Consider the Moon is traversing through Libra (Thula)
3. The query will be related to the Karakathuva of the planet posited in Libra (Thula) (Present). If there are no planets in Libra, then it will be either about a subject related to Libra Sign/Rasi or its Lord Venus.

4. The query may also be based on the Karakathuva of the planets aspect Libra (Thula) Sign/Rasi (Present)
5. It might have been about the Karakathuvas of the Sign/Rasi crossed over by the transit Moon or the planet/s posited in it. (Past instances).
6. The future actions of the querist will depend upon the natal (birth) chart planet and its Karakathuvas about to be touched by the transit Moon.

In short…

It is the relativity established/to be established by the transit Moon with the natal (birth) chart planets in the order of

1. The planet it has already met/crossed over
2. The planet is about to meet/touch and cross over.
3. The planets that aspect it.
4. The planet/s it will touch in the future/next or next Sign/Rasi.
5. The planet/s currently conjoined the Moon in transit at present.

When an analysis of the above five points is done, the result will be the problems that might have been faced by the querist.

If the transit Moon finds no planets in the Sign/Rasi it had moved in, the past and future results can be identified by moving the transit Moon to a square behind or ahead to judge the results. Along with this, other transitory planets along with their positions should be correlated to arrive at the intensity of the problems.

The planets posited in the 2nd house and trines (5th and 9th house) of the transiting Moon signify the future of the querist.

While the planet posited in the 2nd house to the transit Moon indicates the immediate next happenings, those in the trines (5th and 9th house) point at something that may crop up after months.

Chandra Naadi

More for You as hints

Four years rolled by from the day of published 'Chandra Naadi' in English and so have the additions to my experience. I would like to share the same with my readers in the form of small hints that will be useful in their application or perusal using 'Chandra Naadi'.

A humpty number of questions keep popping up from 'n' the number of clients and it is the absolute grace of God and our preceptor who rescue and lead us in those tight situations. I will have goosebumps when my clients remain spellbound with tears rolling down their cheeks on hearing my predictions about hitherto unanswered questions they had for years.

I firmly believe that these hints will be of much use when you are in confusion or glitches to decide. You can find most of the phrases mentioned here might not have found a place in the first edition. I have given some example charts with necessary planetary positions without keeping complete details to maintain the secrecy of my clients. However, the details and explanation given by me will be sufficient to understand the concept and result of the query raised.

I will be happy if the readers of this book get an enlightened and enhanced knowledge about 'Chandra Naadi' in due course of time. The response received for my first edition of 'Chandra Naadi' from all types of readers including prominent astrologers elated me and kept me energised to do more in the field of Astrology.

Business or Profession Indicated by Planetary Combinations

Sun + Jupiter + Moon

The food industry and in places under a roof (Without sweating out)

Sun + Jupiter + Mars

Higher managerial positions, Temples and Jobs connected with the Temple maintenance of Family God, Leading and Organizing public functions.

Sun + Saturn

Senior Accounts Officer, Politics, Family Business, Bone treatments.

Sun + Jupiter + Mercury

Hereditary business/Profession, Manager of Temple Accounts.

Moon + Ketu + Jupiter + Mars

Silk thread manufacturer, Cotton thread manufacturer, and a small vendor in Temples.

Moon + Mars + Saturn

Logistics and Vehicles, Agriculturists, Drivers, Textiles, and Machineries.

Moon + Venus + Mercury

Textile Business and Marketing, Cosmetics and Perfume sellers.

Moon + Venus

Lawyers, Artists, Textile Businesses, Bankers, and dealers of all advanced communication equipment.

Moon + Saturn

Provision stores, self-employment, cool drinks, Salt, Milk, Traders, Oil business, Hotel management and eatables, Banana and other leaves sales, and Food items.

Jupiter + Venus

Finance and Financial centres, Jewellery shops, garments and ornaments.

Jupiter + Venus + Rahu

Cinema, Cell phones and accessories, Computers and accessories, Films, Electronics, Shadow and nighttime illegal businesses, yellow magazines, and magazines that have nude and obscene posters.

Jupiter + Sun

Political leadership, administrative management.

Strength of natal planets during transit

We have to understand how to calculate and use the strength of natal (birth) chart planets during their transit. e.g. The exalted Venus in Pisces possesses 100% strength but loses 50% while it occupies Taurus in transit though it is ruling. It further reduces to 25% when debilitated in Virgo. While Venus loses its Karakathuva characteristics in transit, it does not fail to extend its Bhavaga results.

In similar lines, their strength depends upon the friendlier, neutral or inimical nature of the planets it conjoins or associates in the Sign/Rasi during transit.

Punarpoo

What is meant by Punarpoo?

The planetary position that turns a present event upside down is termed Punarpoo.

1. Any event may turn upside down at the last moment.
2. Turn off life events at the last minute.
3. Marriages will get stopped right at the time of tying the knot.
4. Cancellation or violation of Agreements entered for the sale of land or house at the last hour.
5. 99.9% Cancellation of scheduled events at the zero hour.
6. Events scheduled vanish as a dream or occurrence of an event like a dream.

The planetary combination that propels Punarpoo to act.

The powerful combination of the Moon and Saturn activates Punarpoo. The combination of the Moon and Saturn in any form in a Sign/Rasi, in an asterism (star), each other's aspect or through conjunction. The intensity varies according to the form of the combination and the results should be declared after scrutiny.

Punarpoo and Marriage

One of my close friends came to consult me for his son's marriage.

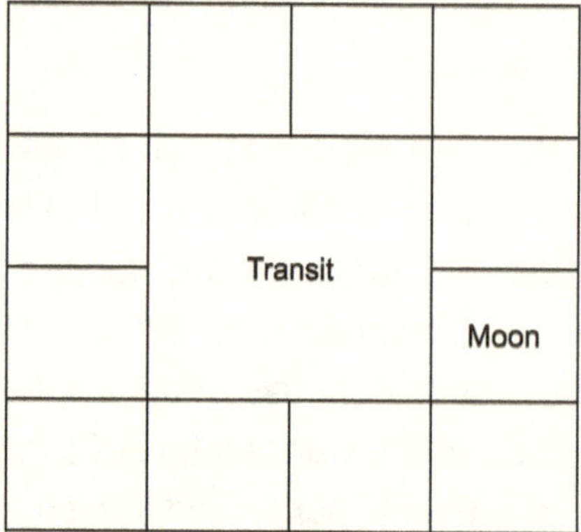

In the above chart of the native, Saturn and the Moon are posited in Leo, and the Purva Phalguni (Pooram) star and Ketu are in the ascendant. They approached on a day ruled by an asterism star in Leo Sign/Rasi as indicated by the transit Moon.

The Punarpoo exists very strongly in the 7th house in the natal (birth) chart, and the transit Moon establishes it. Hence, I told them that Punarpoo is sure to act and anything may happen at the last moment until tying the knot and stoppage of the marriage.

My friend came back to invite me to the marriage on a day when Punarpoo prevailed causing botheration about my earlier statement. I again reminded them about the blemish of Punarpoo. 40 days ahead of the marriage, an uncle of the bridegroom died.

My friend called me up at 5.30 early morning on the day of marriage while I was at Hosur, causing mental tension and establishing the evolution of Punarpoo again.

Notes:

On marriage day, there was a public bundh around Tirupur only insisting on the implementation of prohibition preventing many people from attending the marriage function.

However, the marriage took place after so many hurdles.

Now, the married couple are leading a heavenly life as all the hindrances caused by Punarpoo are over and good days are promised.

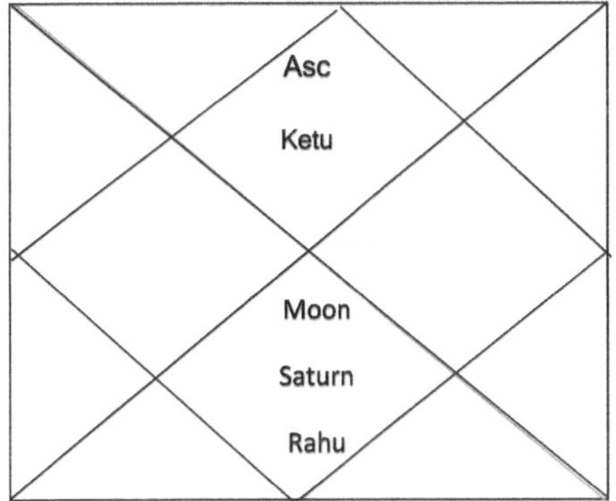

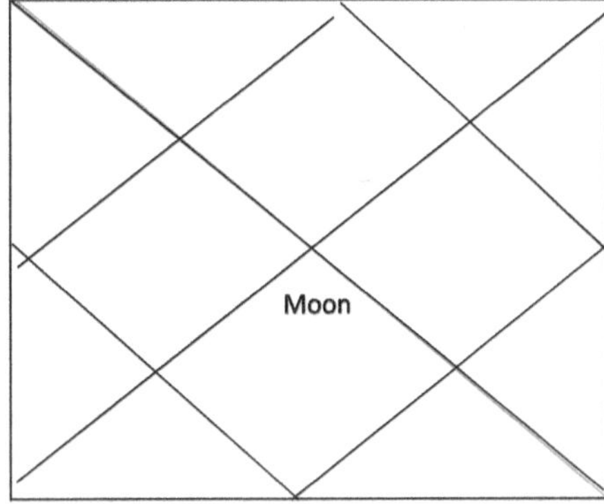

Some hints about owning/buying of Landed Properties

Significators of Land and Buildings

Mars

Vacant land, Houses, Land (Agricultural and Non-Agricultural), Wealth

Sun + Mars

Paternal properties, big buildings

Moon + Mars

Maternal properties

Mercury + Mars

Vacant land, business places, shops, establishments and buildings

Jupiter + Mars

Most valuable places, Temple land, properties of great grandfather, Children's properties.

Venus + Mars

Business establishments in a busy crowded area, properties in the name of spouse, wealth in the name of women.

Saturn + Mars

Hereditary properties, ancestral properties, and place of work.

Rahu + Mars

Encumbered properties, illegal properties owned by litigants.

Ketu + Mars

Properties which are under litigation and legal proceedings, irregular properties.

All the above may be used along with the Karakathuvas of other planets in declaring the results according to the present situation and merit.

Notes:

The combination of the Moon + Mars in the natal (birth) chart of a native will keep inducing him to buy land and residential buildings – the Karakathuvas relating to Mars – and this thought will fructify during a favourable Maha Dasa (Dasa), Anthar Dasa (Bukthi) and transit.

When the query is about land...

There are many differences between the aspect of Mars when posited alone in a Sign/Rasi and while combined/conjoined with Jupiter or Rahu/Ketu. The aspect of Lonely Mars indicates an unencumbered land (land free from problems) and his association with Jupiter will bring fortune to the native through the purchased land. The association of Mars with Rahu brings excessive problems and Ketu legal implications through the land to the natives.

When the query is about the marriage of a female native...

The Lonely Mars refers to her marriage to a person with a calm nature and a life without any problems.

Jupiter associated Mars assures fortune and a harmonious, happy life to the females through their husbands. The Mars + Rahu combination plays havoc and fear in the married life of the female natives while The Mars + Ketu combination indicates disputes, legal implications and unexpected multiple problems through their husbands after marriage.

Information regarding the purchase and sale of landed properties:

When a query regarding the possible time of purchase or sale of landed properties, we have to answer based on planetary revolution time as period.

- The sun moves at a steady speed and hence the action will be during the normal course of time.
- The Moon is fast-moving but with some temptations. Speedy actions give room for suspicion. Actions will be at a fast phase.
- Mars is also a fast-moving planet indicating speedy actions.
- Mercury's association gives radical changes in results. But things will be as per plan.
- Jupiter extends delayed but results for sure.
- Venus extends quick results in the absence of financial constraints.
- Saturn is a slow planet and any actions related to it will be delayed or deferred due to time factors.
- Rahu, Ketu, and Manthi cause hurdles in any action. Difficulties and problems including legal implications need to be faced and none of the actions will go as easily as planned.

These things should be borne in mind by the astrologer before declaring the probable time of completion of any task.

Nil Results by the Transit Moon

The Transit Moon will not indicate any results when its motion is not influenced by any natal (birth) chart planet/s by conjunction or aspect.

1. The visitors may say that they peeped in to have a glance at the Astrologer on their casual walk along the road.
2. Some clients may ask things that are improbable in their life. A client who is earning 50Rupees a week inquired whether he can buy a new Car.
3. Those who do not own even a piece of land would like to know when they will construct a house and whether they will get any bounty/treasure during the breaking.
4. A female who was declared barren and impossible to inherit children through any medical application, approached me with a question as to how many children she will have.

My answers to all the above questions are the same. When the transit Moon is not connected with any natal (birth) chart planet by any means like, conjoin, aspect, positioning of the planets in the asterisms of the Lord of the Sign/Rasi occupied by the transit Moon. I will ask them to pray to their family God and return after some time.

I will be silent when none of the natal Karaka planets are relevant to the transit Moon.

Chandra Naadi and Exchange of Houses

For a native to realise the benefits through planets under the exchange of their houses, the transit Moon should pass over such houses or receive the aspect of the planets posited there and not any other time.

Saturn			
Jupiter	Saturn Jupiter Exchange		
		Moon (Transit)	

50%	100%	50%	
100%	Saturn's Benefits in Signs After Exchange of Houses by Saturn and Jupiter		
			100%
50%	100%		50%

The three houses Taurus, Virgo, and Sagittarius which receive the aspect of Saturn's 3rd, 7th, and 10th along with Pisces where it is posited get 50% results and 100% to the signs Aries, Leo, Scorpio and Aquarius after the exchange of houses.

When will the result due to the Exchange of Houses can be felt?

The results due to the Exchange of Houses will take effect only during the transit of the planets when either of the planets traverses over the Signs/Rasis they exchange or aspect.

Birth   Transit

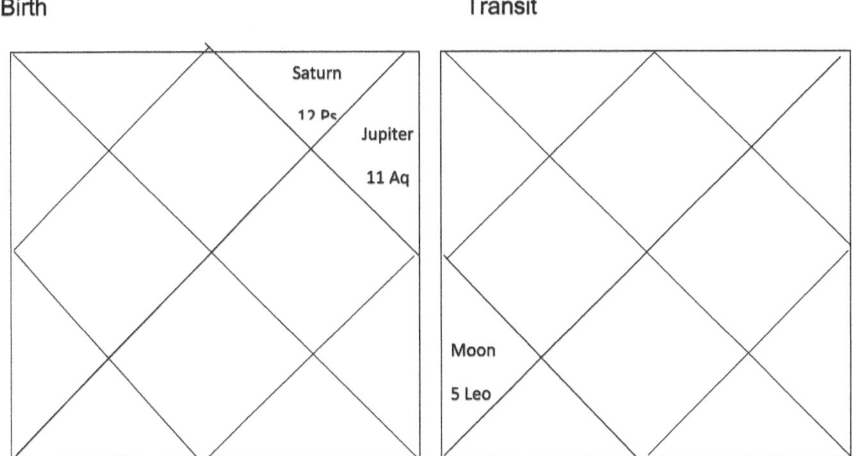

Exchange of houses by Retrograded auspicious (benefic) planets:

When benefic planets retrograde and exchange their houses, the bitterness exhibited by them or the results of their Karaka and Bhava are very ticklish and beyond revealing. At times it gives unbearable displeasure and bitterness beyond explanation.

Such a situation or position can better be described as misfortune instead of fortune as the impact is greater.

Some hints to facilitate judgement:

1. When a native turns up for a consultation on a day of transit Moon traversing in the Same Sign/Rasi where three or more planets are conjoined, it indicates that the native is facing enormous problems and if he is mentally strong, he will withstand the problems. If he is mentally weak, he will attempt to commit suicide or elope from his residence.

2. Only the transit Moon is responsible for transforming the benefits resulting through planetary combinations in the natal (birth) chart. Even if there are several combinations present in the chart, the benefits will be through the one in which the transit Moon establishes contact.

3. On many occasions same planetary combinations extend different results gender-wise which means it is not the same for Gents and ladies.

4. The native absolves the benefic or malefic results depending upon the association/conjunction/aspect embraced by the transit Moon.

E.g.

1. Take, for instance, the planetary combination of the Moon and Mars under the aspect of Saturn. Here the natives will enjoy the Karagathuvas of Mars which are, land, buildings, vehicles etc., very easily. But as Saturn's aspect is also present, the natives will lose before enjoying them.

2. A native waited for 10 years to marry his sister's daughter (Karakathuva of Mars) but in vain.

3. A land was purchased in haste but forced to sell without using it.

4. All brothers of a native remain for namesake and inactive as Saturn as the foe of Mars forbids the benefits due from the association of the Moon and Mars.

5. The aspect of the conjoined Jupiter and Moon over the transit Moon propels the native to have his wants satisfied by himself and remain selfish. Both planets denote the closure of the issues.

The Transit Moon's Activity in Chandra Naadi

In Chandra Naadi, the results are accurate and swift when the transit Moon is in Waxing status. It is slow during the waning stage of the transit Moon.

The conjunction/aspect of Mars with the transit Moon extends steady activities.

When the transit Moon conjoins the Sun or receives its aspect, its activities are steady but stretched.

Rahu when associated with the transit Moon in the form of conjunction or control, causes fear to the native and forces him to move away from the scene immediately.

Ketu's position in the above position projects critical, unidentifiable problems/diseases, and indecisive status to the native.

Rahu and Ketu are shadow planets and the Premiers of shadow life activities. All illegal activities, businesses, and unlawful actions are monitored and headed by these two nodes Rahu and Ketu. When Rahu and Ketu join hands with Saturn, it will not be exposed and remain in the dark.

The luminaries brighten the actions of Rahu and Ketu. Hence, the natives with the Sun or Moon's combination with Rahu/Ketu in their natal (birth) chart get their actions exposed in public.

Rahu and Ketu's association with any planet returns a definite good or bad result.

Role of Retrograde Planets

Retrograded planets extend unforgettable painful moments in the lives of the natives.

For instance, retrograded Saturn indicates such unforgettable pain as any of the Karakathuvas of Saturn detailed as under.

1. The natives worry about their inability to worship their family God.
2. They will feel contactless with their uncles – elder or younger brothers of their father.
3. Failures in their actions.
4. Their actions regarding the purchase and sale of old/vintage landed properties, buildings, and objects.
5. Some natives may worry about their Gender (Saturn is an Eunuch in nature).
6. Cheating or misbehaviour nature of the servants/subordinates despite paying a good salary on time.
7. Non-receipt of wages/salary on time after proper work.

The above statements indicate that the retrograded planets never deny any results but delay them. They do not allow the natives to enjoy the benefits in full as they tangle by taking away their Karakathuva results after giving them earlier.

When a native finds retrograded Venus in his natal (birth) chart, his wife often goes away to her mother's house over family disputes else his married sister returns to his house with some demands.

- Retrograded Venus refers to wives, elder sisters and elderly women.
- If the native's wife goes back to her mother's house citing family disputes, his sister will not return.

- When the native's elder sister returns to his house with some demands, his wife will not go to her mother's house despite family disputes.

Though a planet possesses two different Karakathuvas, only one of them gains strength and impacts the native keeping the other in mute condition.

Significators of Mars

Mars is the common significator of both Vehicles and Machinery. It varies according to the planets Mars conjoined with. In Chandra Naadi, this classification helps to identify the area, job, work, business, and education the native may be connected to.

Mars + Sun

Machinery that is connected with Government Jobs e.g. Road Rollers

Mars + Moon

Fast-moving machines, agricultural machines like tractors, cooking machines like Grinders, public utility machines and vehicles.

Mars + Mercury

Newspaper, Magazine Printing Machines, Micro and hand-sized machines, Gadgets, and instruments.

Mars + Jupiter

Machines that are used for the basic needs of the General Public, life-saving machines and instruments in hospitals like Ventilators, ECG, Echo etc.,

Mars + Venus

Luxurious Machines. Machines that work in Air-conditioned rooms, Scientific instruments and Computers.

Mars + Saturn

Mounted big roller Machines, Cranes, Old Machines, Garbage and Sewage cleaners.

Mars + Rahu/Ketu

Machines that operate through chain and conveyor belt systems, Sea Saws, Sewing Machines, Cutting machines, Mills, Windmills, Polythene manufacturing machines, Rubber machinery, and Road engines. Etc.,

Mars + The Sun + Rahu

Boulder breaking machinery used in Stone Quarries.

Mars + Venus + Saturn

Building machines, Construction machinery.

As Mars indicates Machines, its presence along with the planets it is associated with or aspected by in Signs/Rasis or asterisms signifies different types of machinery. The intense knowledge about the Karakathuvas of planets and bhava enlarges the predictive astrology to a greater extent.

Depleted Strength of Jupiter

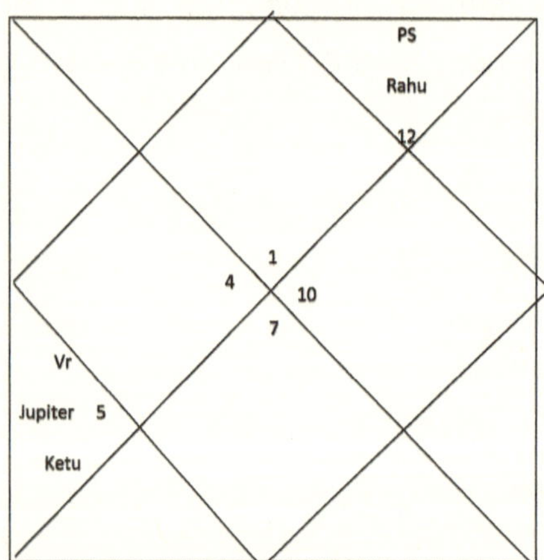

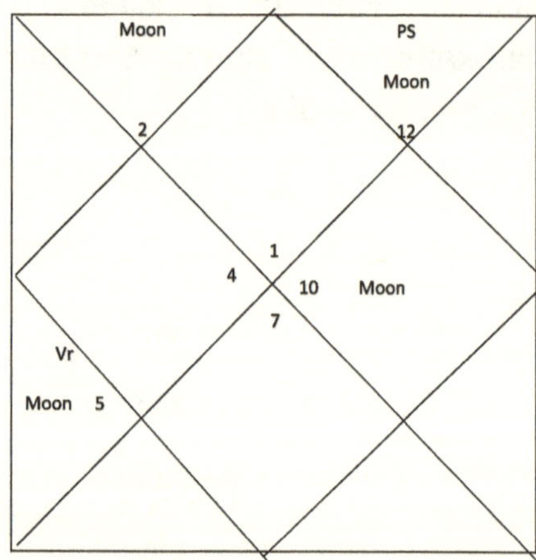

In the above natal (birth) chart on the left, Jupiter at 159° is afflicted by Ketu at 162° moving towards it. Though the transit Moon in general terms believed to extend beneficial results through natal Jupiter's aspect, here it is not due to Jupiter's affliction. This indicates that the native will never receive a fortune of Jupiter's aspect.

Hints in prediction:

The combined status of Jupiter and Ketu will cause debts to the natives and transactions involving money will be tougher and problematic. Monetary transactions will cause headaches for these natives. But this planetary combination is good for spiritual serenity and search for peace in a holy way. These results can be declared during the Moon's transit.

Change in Planetary Karkathuvas According to its Bhavagas

It should be reckoned that a planet extends its beneficial or malefic results according to the planet it is associated with.

It equally varies depending upon the Bhavagas and Sign/Rasi Characteristics detailed below:

Venus in 1st House – Self Personal) beautification

Venus in 2nd House – Charming face, Eyes

Venus in 3rd House – Personal pleasures (sensual/sexual)

Venus in 4th House – Mother, Luxury Vehicles

Venus in 5th House – Baby girls or female children of maternal Uncles

Venus in 6th House – Diabetes and hormone imbalances

Venus in 7th House – Wife/Spouse

Venus in 8th House – Insult/disgrace through money and women

Venus in 9th House – Father's influence, Wealth

Venus in 10th House – Investment in Business

Venus in 11th House – Sisters of the Native

Venus in 12th House – Personal friend and personal secrets/relations

A planet remits its results based on the bhava it is posited. For instance, Venus in the 4th House swaps its results depending upon its position in Movable, Fixed or Dual Signs.

4th house Venus in Movable Sign refers to Luxury Vehicle

4th House Venus in Fixed Sign indicates Life-saving drugs/medicine.

4th House Venus in Dual Sign refers to Cattle and Coparceners.

Hence an extensive knowledge of planetary Karakathuvas is the prime requisite for an astrologer to give precise results.

Planetary Strength During Transit

The following table shows that only the transit Mars decides the strength and weakness of the natal Mars.

	Signs of Transit Mars	Result %
	Cancer	50%
	Scorpio	75%
Natal (Birth) Chart Mars Is in Aries (Mesha)	Capricorn	200%
	Gemini with Ketu	50%
	Aquarius with Rahu	-100%
	With Jupiter	+200%

The above table indicates that whenever the transit Mars acquires strength the natal Mars too gains strength and weakens when the transit Mars becomes weak in its Transit. The above value simplifies our approach to prediction.

As the strength or weakness of the natal (birth) chart Mars gets changed by the influence of transit Mars,

1. The Karakathuvas of Mars gets stronger at times
2. The Karakathuvas of Mars gets weaker at some other times
3. Be inactive or with Null strength during other periods.

The above status of Mars implies that a native's relationship with his siblings in similar situations

- Be more attached and affectionate
- Be fighting
- Remain without any contact for sometime
- Support his brother by fulfilling his requirements.

The above change in the behaviour of a native is nothing but the mood the transit Mars creates based on its relationship with the natal (birth) chart Mars.

The position of Mars in the natal (birth) chart is the fundamental character of the native with his siblings and the transit Mars exhibits his change of behaviour with them from time to time in line with the strength or weakness between the natal (birth) and transit planets.

The natal planets are like the roots of a tree while the transiting planets are the external growth.

In other words, the relationship between the transit Moon and

- ✓ The planet aspect of the transit Moon
- ✓ The positional strength or weakness of the planet
- ✓ The position of the transit Moon should be weighed upon.

Most of the queries raised during the contact of the transit Moon with Rahu/Ketu nodes are about

1. Products/objects/people lost
2. About the incidents that bothered their mind.
3. Sorrow/distress
4. Legal entanglements/litigation they are facing.
5. Separations/Parting off

Even if their queries are about any auspicious occasions, they only indicate interruptions or stoppages. In all Rahu/Ketu are at their best in causing distress and disruptions giving an unhappy ending.

According to my research, it is imperative that though the natal Rahu/Ketu sometimes extend some benefits or fortune, the transit Rahu or Ketu never does any good.

If we evaluate the power of malefic

- The Lord of the 8th house (Ashtamathipathi) is 10 times more powerful than the evil doer (Bhadagathipathi – 11th house lord or 9th house lord or the 7th house lord for Movable, Fixed or Dual Signs.
- Ketu is 10 times more powerful than the Lord of the 8th house.
- Rahu is 10 times more powerful than Ketu
- Manthi does the evilest as it is 10 times more powerful than Rahu

Brief Hints about Retrograded Planets

1. Retrograded planets will cause mental torture to the native through their planetary, bhava and lordship Karakathuvas.
2. Retrograded planets cause jealousy in the minds of the natives.
3. They will always be ready to cause trouble when challenged.
4. Rahu and Ketu will not impact retrograded planets.
5. Retrograded planets will gain strength when they conjoin the nodes Rahu/Ketu and will shower sudden fortunes through their Karakathuvas.
6. Retrograded planets in transit will extend their results once they become direct.
7. Retrograded planets will delay their fortunes and benefits but never deny it.

A planet extends its benefit based on,

- The characteristics of the Signs where it is posited
- The characteristics of the asterism in which it is posited
- The characteristics of the planet it is associated with.
- The characteristics of the planet that aspect it.

We will experience and be thrilled to note the results extended by the planets when we analyse multiple natal charts. A planet will throw both beneficial and malefic aspects from the same sign it occupies.

Some Hints Related to Queries

- Why do we use natal (birth) chart?
- Why do we use the Transit (of planets) chart?
- What is the use of Maha Dasa (Dasa), Anthar Dasa (Bukthi) and Prithyanthar Dasa (Antharam)?

These questions will arise in the minds of so many querists. Many might use them without their proper application or how to relate them. Please find the explanation for the same as under:

1. Whenever a question arises as to 'Why'? use the natal (birth) chart. (This gives the thought about an action)
2. Whenever the question about time (as to when?) arises analyse the present Transit chart of planets (To set the action in motion or begin the action)
3. To assess how long the process will continue, look at the current Maha Dasa (Dasa), Anthar Dasa (Bukthi), and Prithyanthar Dasa (Antharam) in operation.

E.g. The thought about constructing a house will arise depending on the natal (birth) chart and the current planetary transit will initiate to start the project and the Maha Dasa (Dasa), Anthar Dasa (Bukthi), and Prityanthar Dasa (Antharam) will indicate the probable period of completion of the construction of the house.

A Planet reveals the character and a Bhava indicates relevant action

The transit chart should be correlated for planetary position and the present Maha Dasa (Dasa), and Anthar Dasa (Bukthi) should be checked for Bhavaga results.

Roll of Maha Dasa (Dasa), and Anthar Dasa (Bukthi)

Results based on natal (birth) chart:

> ➢ The current planetary transit will never overrule the Maha Dasa (Dasa) of Anthar Dasa (Bukthi)
> ➢ The present Maha Dasa (Dasa), and Anthar Dasa (Bukthi) will not override the current transit of planetary movements.

Both will work in tandem and will not act individually.

Let us compare this to a motor vehicle. The four-wheeler is the Maha Dasa (Dasa), and Anthar Dasa (Buktthi) and the Driver of the vehicle is pointed to the current planetary transit. The road or path in which the vehicle is driven depends on the natal (birth) chart.

in a nutshell, there should be a path or a road to drive, a vehicle to travel and a driver to drive the vehicle. Without the combination of all of these three, a result could not be arrived at.

Kindly experience the results of my research with the natal (birth) charts you may come across in your life to know the real.

Planetary Comparison – in Joint Natal (Birth) Charts

Some more hints are given here to analyse multiple natal (birth) charts (by comparing them) using 'Chandra Naadi'.

There are no big differences in the basic rules used.

Planetary comparison:

1. If Saturn is placed in the *same* sign of a female natal (birth) chart in which the Sun is posited in the natal (birth) chart of a male, it will delay them in begetting a child or Progeny. (Delay in Child Birth).

2. When comparing two natal (birth) charts, if the Moon is placed in the *same* sign of one in which Rahu of the other is posited, the person with the Moon in his sign will fear the person with Rahu and also be humiliated by him.

3. When comparing two natal (birth) charts, if the Moon is placed in the *same* sign of one in which Ketu of the other is posited, the person with the Moon in his sign will face mental torture, tension and legal problems through the one who has Ketu in the same sign.

4. When comparing two natal (birth) charts, if the Moon is placed in the *same* sign of one in which Saturn of the other is posited, the person with the Moon in his sign will face heavy burden by the one who has Saturn there. The Moon – Load bearer. Saturn – Load imparter.

5. When comparing two natal (birth) charts, if the Moon is placed in the *same* sign of one in which Jupiter of the other is posited, the person with the Moon in his sign will be very fortunate and the native will be well taken care of by the one who has Jupiter there.

6. When comparing two natal (birth) charts, if Rahu is placed in the *same* sign of one in which Saturn of the other is posited, the venture they both engaged in will face an abrupt end face closure. Both will not have any consensus in their decisions.

7. When comparing two natal (birth) charts, if Ketu is placed in the *same* sign of one in which Saturn of the other is posited, the venture they both engaged in will face litigations and legal implications leading to separation.

8. When comparing two natal (birth) charts if a friendlier planet is placed in the *same* sign in which a benefic planet is posited, the native will receive beneficial results.

9. When comparing two natal (birth) charts if an inimical planet is placed in the *same* sign in which a malefic planet is posited, the native will receive the worst results.

10. It is my conclusive result that only depending on the planets posited in the same *sign* of the two persons whose charts are under comparison, their joint business venture, marriage, etc., will happen.

11. It is better to see the placement of Rahu or Ketu in the *same* sign of One person in which Rahu of the Other is posited. This will either magnify the problem or cease to exist.

12. When comparing two natal (birth) charts, if Rahu/Ketu is placed in the *same* sign of one in which Mars of the other is posited, both natives should not have any relationships/connection or venture in the Karakathuvas of Mars like land, buildings, houses, and vehicles as it will cause immense problems between them. This will be highlighted by the Transit Moon.

Miserable Transit

Which transit causes misery in the life of a native?

When the malefic transit planets come into contact with the natal (birth) chart planets, miserable or unbearable tragic events occur in the life of a native.

1. Transit of malefic planets like Rahu – Ketu – Saturn or Mars over natal (birth) chart Rahu's position in degrees.
2. Transit of malefic planets like Rahu – Ketu – Saturn or Mars over natal (birth) chart Ketu's position in degrees.

If this conjunction occurs during the Maha Dasa (Dasa) or Anthar Dasa (Bukthi) of the same malefic planets, the distress will be cruel.

Example:

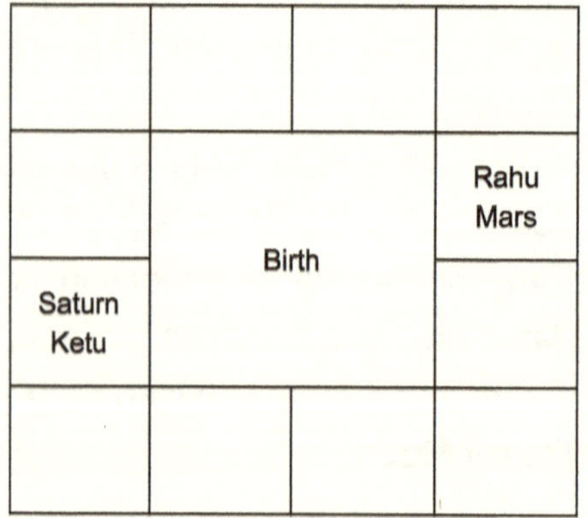

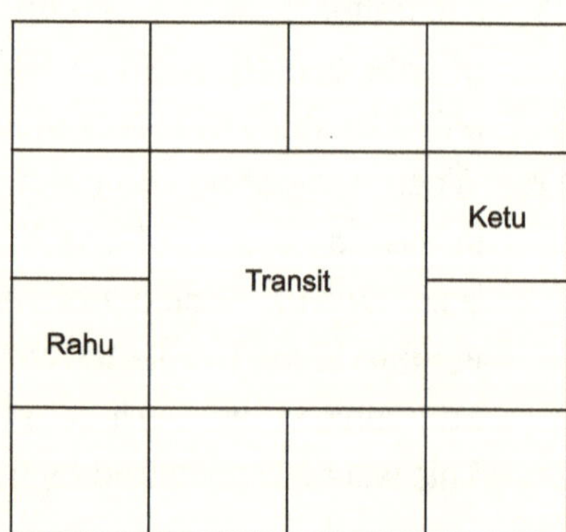

The above native was running Saturn Maha Dasa (Dasa) – Rahu Anthar Dasa (Bukthi) – Ketu Prityanthar Dasa (Antharam). His marriage broke away in three days as the malefic planets Rahu/Ketu were transiting over the natal (birth) chart malefic Rahu/Ketu and the Maha Dasa (Dasa) and Anthar Dasa (Bukthi) adding fuel to the fire making it crueller.

Is Gender discrimination essential?

Yes. It is very important. While declaring results like uterus problems, menstruation problems or Cervix, it is important to distinguish the gender as male or female.

Likewise, should we consider the age?

Yes. We should.

While considering the Karakathuvas of Saturn,

3. It should be reckoned as a health issue in the case of children
4. Dullness or slump in education
5. Job during the Middle Ages
6. Business or Profession in later years
7. Diseases in old age

For the question about the time factor, only a delay in all events should be considered.

Combusted Planet

During the identical positioning of planets in the natal (birth) chart and the transit, there will be some minor differences in the movement of the transit Moon which has to be carefully observed.

The chart is that of a male referred by my friend. In both natal (birth) and transit Venus is combusted through its proximity to the Sun.

The Outer square denotes the Transit

The transit Moon is about to contact Venus. According to 'Chandra Naadi'…

In a male chart, the contact of the transit Moon with combusted Venus indicates

1. Everlasting problems through women causing mental worries
2. Disgrace in marriage
3. Love failures
4. Sufferings to the native through the Karakathuvas of Venus
5. Disgrace and distress faced due to non-receipt of outstanding money.
6. Unnatural death of sisters and paternal/maternal aunts
   This will be the subject matter of queries that may be raised.

Both natal (birth) Venus and transit Venus are on the path of the transit Moon. Hence, the probable question that may be raised be

1. Marital disgrace or separation of wife
2. Non-receipt of dues

   The querist informed me that

   - His wife got separated from him four years ago and his attempt to marry again failed due to problems.
   - His Company is due to pay his four months' salary.

The querist wanted to know whether this position would change.

'Chandra Naadi' has established the probable question accurately.

To get the answer to the query, the Maha Dasa (Dasa) and Anthar Dasa (Bukthi) in operation both as per the natal (birth) chart and the transit Moon should be computed and compared.

Fructification time of the event:

1. If anyone lord of Maha Dasa MD (Dasa), Anthar Dasa AD (Bukthi) or Prithyanthar Dasa PAD (Antharam) at the time of birth presently represents as lord of either of Maha Dasa (Dasa), Anthar Dasa (Bukthi) or Prityanthar Dasa (Antharam) as per the transit Moon (Current), then the native will get a beneficial result.
2. E.g. At Birth MD Venus AD Saturn PAD Jupiter
3. During Transit MD Venus AD Jupiter PAD Saturn
4. In addition to the above rules, only when the transit Jupiter throws its aspect over the relative Karaka Planet, the result will be complete and in full.
5. For a querist to get a positive answer to his question, either the transit Moon or the Karaka lord relating to the particular question should receive the aspect of transit Jupiter.
6. The answer will be negative or the querist will face hurdles in his object if the transit Moon is either associated with Rahu/Ketu in the sign or Rahu/Ketu is posited in the sign next to the transit Moon indicating that the transit Moon will touch them immediately.

All the above four rules are 'Golden Rules' to determine the schedule for the fructification of the events.

Now let us look at the prediction part to the two questions put forth by the querist which are:

1. His wife got separated from him four years ago and his attempt to marry again failed due to problems.
2. His Company is due to pay his four months' salary.

At the time of Birth, the native was running

- Venus MD,
- Saturn AD, and
- Jupiter PAD.

On the day of transit Moon was over Purva Phalguni (Pooram) star

- MD – Venus
- AD – Jupiter
- PAD – Saturn

Both the natal and transit MD, AD, and PAD lords are in sync.

➢ The transit Maha Dasa MD (Dasa) lord has become the Maha Dasa MD (Dasa) lord at birth.

➢ The combined association of Jupiter, Saturn and Venus during their transit extends 100% positive results which are confirmed in this case assuring ultimate success to the querist.

The results stand partitioned as below to give 100% positive results.

33% to Maha Dasa MD (Dasa) lord

33% to Anthar Dasa AD (Bukthi) lord

33% to Prityanthar Dasa PAD (Antharam) lord

The querist is a Male, and his Kalathra Karaka lord is Venus. During his transit, Jupiter will conjoin Venus in Aquarius after 19.12.2009 assuring success in January 2010.

As the transit Mon in Leo does not face any evil mongers in the next two signs, the querist is assured of his remarriage and receipt of the money due.

The querist again called me over the phone on 28-12-2009 and informed me that the remarriage prospects are high and are about to be completed.

He came back again to meet me in 2015 for the naming ceremony of his second child.

Chandra Naadi and Chandrashtamam (Transit Moon in 8ᵗʰ House)

Every month the transit Moon passes over the 8ᵗʰ house from the ascendant invariably causing immense distress to every human irrespective of their caste and creed. But it varies every month depending upon its relativity concerning other planets in transit. **The changes are based on two factors. 1) The transit Moon's passing over the standard 8ᵗʰ house from the ascendant. 2) The impact caused by the impact of the transit position of the 8ᵗʰ house lord over the transit Moon and the 8ᵗʰ house.**

Impact of the 8ᵗʰ house lord (the lord of the house indicated by the transit Moon from the Ascendant aka Chandrashtamam) in all the 12 houses along with its lordship sovereign characteristics.

In the 1ˢᵗ house or Ascendant.

As this house happens to be the 12ᵗʰ house to the 2ⁿᵈ house representing money and family matters, on the evil day of 'Chandrashtama' or 'the Moon's transit in 8ᵗʰ house', there will be a) loss of money b) moving out of the family to outstations c) engaging in deeds that lead to partition in the family) e} unkept promises of expenditures f) becoming a cause of partner to suffer humiliation. Even mental tension will result from unrelated incidents.

In the 2ⁿᵈ house

As this house becomes the 12ᵗʰ house to the 3ʳᵈ house, 6ᵗʰ bhava to the 9ᵗʰ bhava and 8ᵗʰ bhava to the 7ᵗʰ bhava, on the evil day of 'Chandrashtama' or 'the Moon's transit in 8ᵗʰ house', it will give

a) Cowardice to the native
b) Waste or squander of money through brothers
c) Problems/mental stress through miscommunications/wrong information
d) Wastage/expenditures through communication equipment/ Gadgets

e) Borrowings/expenditures/mental stress through father and paternal relatives

f) Disgrace and humiliation through wife

g) Unexpected fortunes

h) Humiliation due to greed

In the 3rd house

As this house becomes the 12th house to the 4th house, 8th house to the 8th bhava, on the evil day of 'Chandrashtama' or 'the Moon's transit in 8th house', it will give

I. Health issues to the native

II. Troubles around residence

III. Expenditures in the maintenance of residences and orchards

IV. Fear of life

V. Mental stress through expenditures incurred on account of the mother

VI. Bitterness equal to death

VII. Suicidal tendencies

In the 4th house

As this house becomes the 12th house to the 5th house, 8th bhava to the 9th bhava, on the evil day of 'Chandrashtama' or 'the Moon's transit in 8th house', it will give

1. Medical expenses to the Children

2. Problems through Children

3. Pathetic news from hometown/Native

4. No peace at home

5. Ill health/sickness to father

6. Problems through father

7. Unpleasant events during travel

8. Wasteful expenditure in treatment for begetting children medically, like IVF, etc.,

In the 5th house

As this house becomes the 12th house to the 6th house, 8th bhava to the 10th bhava, on the evil day of 'Chandrashtama' or 'the Moon's transit in 8th house', it will give

1. Distress in incidents close to the heart
2. Intension to increase the debt
3. Excessive borrowings to repay the existing debt
4. Humiliation in business or workplace
5. Getting a bad name for an excellent work done

In the 6th house

As this house becomes the 12th house to the 7th house, 8th bhava to the 11th bhava, on the evil day of 'Chandrashtama' or 'the Moon's transit in 8th house', it will give

A. Medical expenses to husband/wife
B. Unnecessary arguments between the couples
C. Misunderstandings between business partners leading to breaking away from partnership
D. Reduction in anticipated profits
E. Dejection in the anticipated events
F. Problems through maternal Uncles and enemies and it is better to avoid meeting them on these days.
G. Brewing unpleasantness as the profit due to the native pass on to others
H. Accrual of enmity with paternal/maternal uncles
I. Separation from friends
J. Medical expenses to friends
K. Controversies with brothers

In the 7th house

As this house becomes the 12th house to the 8th house, 8th bhava to the 12th bhava, on the evil day of 'Chandrashtama' or 'the Moon's transit in 8th house', it will give

1. On this day, Vehicles should be driven carefully
2. There will be embarrassment in monetary transactions
3. Fear of life and bad dreams will crop up
4. Unnecessary medical expenditure
5. Unwanted expenses through others and there will be disgust after expenditures

In the 8th house

As this house becomes the 12th house to the 9th house, 8th bhava to the Ascendant (1st house), on the evil day of 'Chandrashtama' or 'the Moon's transit in 8th house', it will give

✓ Husband/Wife will receive death news
✓ Arguments erupt between couples leading to humiliation
✓ Medical expenses to the father
✓ Mental stress due to father's displacement
✓ Unpleasant news from those returning from foreign trips/Other states
✓ Confusions from long-distance communications

In the 9th house

As this house becomes the 12th house to the 10th house, 8th bhava to the 2nd house, on the evil day of 'Chandrashtama' or 'the Moon's transit in 8th house', it will give

❖ Disappointment through increase in administrative expenses
❖ Melancholy caused by those in other states, foreign countries
❖ Distress about meagre income
❖ Unnecessary worries about family situations

- ❖ Wasteful expenditures in job and business
- ❖ Increase in problems through intervention of family members

In the 10th house

As this house becomes the 12th house to the 11th house, 8th bhava to the 3rd house, on the evil day of 'Chandrashtama' or 'the Moon's transit in 8th house', it will give

- o Distress due to Continuing business without anticipated profit
- o Reduction in profit due to wrong decisions
- o Minor accidents
- o Meeting heavy expenses or big problems even in minor accidents
- o Humiliation to siblings
- o If the natal (birth) chart indicates the sibling's death period, it will likely happen.
- o Distress through actions involving houses let off for rent or through tenants and bitterness with them.
- o Unwarranted disputes and squabbles will emerge.

In the 11th house

As this house becomes the 12th house to the 12th house, 8th bhava to the 4th house, on the evil day of 'Chandrashtama' or 'the Moon's transit in 8th house', it will give

- – There will be reduced profit from business which will become useless.
- – Had it been the death afflicting period for the mother, the death will happen.
- – It will cause accidents and health issues for the mother to undergo medical treatment.
- – Chances of Vehicle theft and burglary at house
- – Good deeds will turn soar
- – Additional borrowings will be made to repay old loans

In the 12th house

As this house becomes the 12th house to the Ascendant (1st house), 8th bhava to the 5th house, on the evil day of 'Chandrashtama' or 'the Moon's transit in 8th house', it will give

- Unnecessary expenditures
- Medical expenses
- Wasteful travel expenses
- Pain due to misunderstandings by children
- Humiliation through children
- Problems in the native village
- Wrong decisions relating to ancestral properties
- Spilling words that hurt the children
- Misunderstandings through adopted children

These are certain repercussions due to the transit of the Moon in the 8th house from the ascendant and the position of the lord of the 8th house in transit. Exercising caution during this period can save you from the impact.

Tara Palam or Auspicious Strengths of Asterisms

Astrology Classifies the strength of asterisms from the birth star of a native as good and bad depending on their placement in numerological order from 1 to 9. The Even number of stars from the birth star – namely 2nd, 4th, 6th, 8th, and 9th – are considered to possess auspicious strength and termed to possess 'Tara Palam' aka 'Positional strength' in general. **But the results of 'Tara Palam' or 'Positional Strength' change depending on the Planets posited in these stars.**

The 2nd star from the 'birth star' will be functional and bestow beneficial results only when NO planets are posited in that star/ asterism. When a planet is positioned in that asterism, the results are only extended by that particular planet. Similarly, in the natal (birth) chart if a planet occupies the 2nd star, it will extend the results of the bhava/sign it occupies during its transit.

Let us assume the birth star is Revathi where the Moon is present and Rahu in the star Aswini.

When the transit Moon passes over the natal Rahu in Aries (star Aswini), the promising financial benefits of the 2nd house cannot be derived but there will be a slump in the economic conditions giving lethal life and bitter incidents.

A planet posited in the designated stars which is supposed to possess 'Tara Palam' or 'Positional strength' alters its beneficial strength and forces its own. This should be carefully considered before declaring the results.

'Chandra Naadi' either increases or decreases the 'Tara Palam' or 'Positional strength'.

Planetary Strength Depending on their Positions

The strength of each planet varies depending on its positional strength in the natal (birth) chart and during transit which includes its placement in their stars.

For instance, let us look at the positional strength of *Mars* as explained by the chart given below:

	1 Mars (Ruling)		
6 Rahu Mars			2 Asc Mars Debilitation
5 Mars @ 27° Exaltation Deep Exaltation 28°			Ketu
	4 Mars (Ruling)	3 Mars (Chithirai)	

Basic positional Strength in Natal (birth) chart

A. Ruling Mars in Aries (Mool Trikon 200%), Scorpio – 100%
B. Exalted Mars in Capricorn – 200%
C. Directional Strength @ 10th house – 300% (Any Ascendant)
D. Debilitated Mars – (Minus strength)
E. Mars in its star – 50%

Now the strength of Mars during Transit

1. Mars in Aries – Directional strength 10th for Cancer Ascendant 300%+ Mool Trikon 200% + Ruling 100% = 600%
2. Debilitation in Cancer – (Minus) 100%
3. Mars in Libra in Chita (Chithirai star – 50%
4. Mars in Scorpio – 100%
5. Mars in Capricorn – 200% + 300% = 500%
6. Mars in Aquarius Rahu moving towards Mars – Complete loss of strength

Aspects of Planets and 'Chandra Naadi'

Rule No. 1

There are many differences in the individual aspects of a planet and its combined aspects with another planet.

Rule No. 2

There are many differences between the individual aspects of a planet and the aspects transmitted over it by another planet.

The Outer square represents the transit chart and the inner square shows the natal (birth) chart

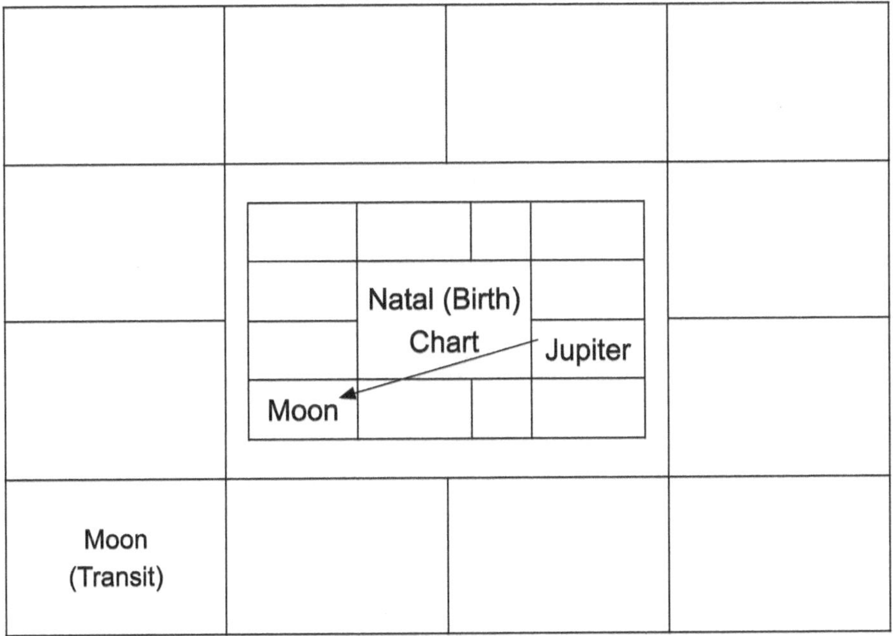

Here Jupiter possesses a pious nature. The transit Moon assures the calm and composed character of the native.

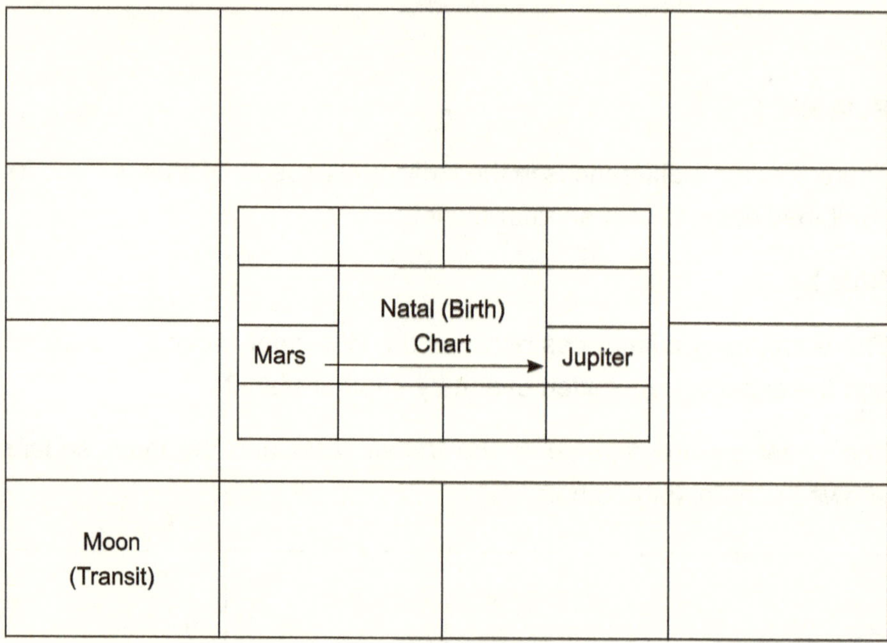

In the above natal (birth) chart Exalted Mars in Capricorn throws its 8th aspect over Jupiter in Leo thereby changing his sattvic nature to a rough one and making him obey his orders but will not listen to him.

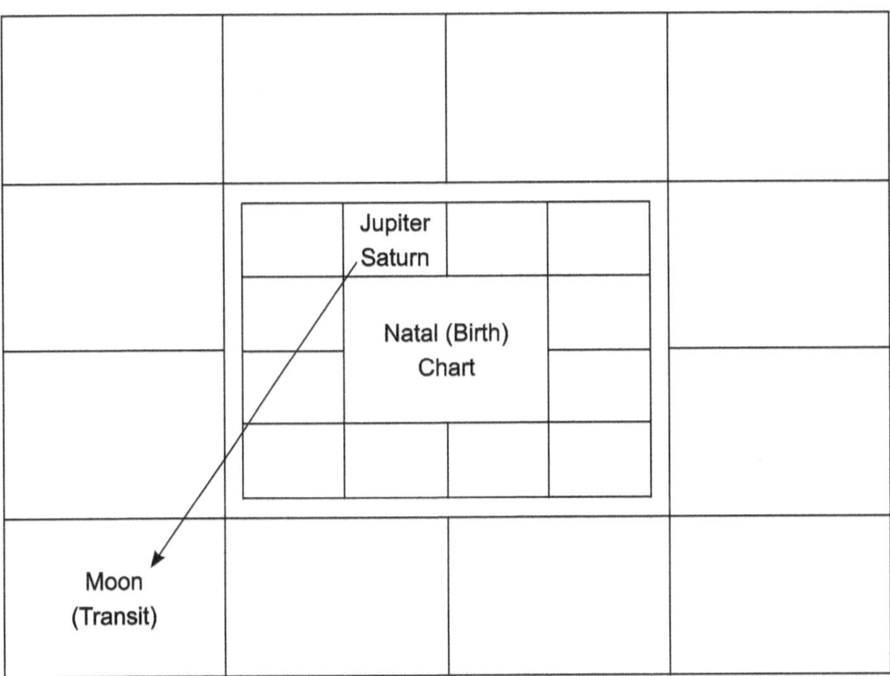

Here Jupiter in Aries of the natal (birth) chart has conjoined debilitated Saturn exhibiting its substandard character and disability.

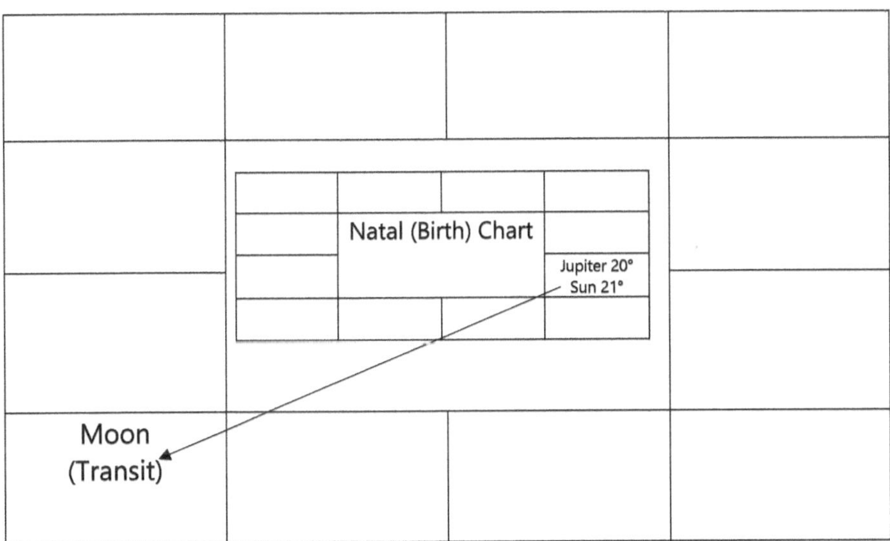

In the above chart Jupiter at 20° in Leo is combusted by its proximity to the Sun at 21° blocking and disabling the beneficial aspects of Jupiter.

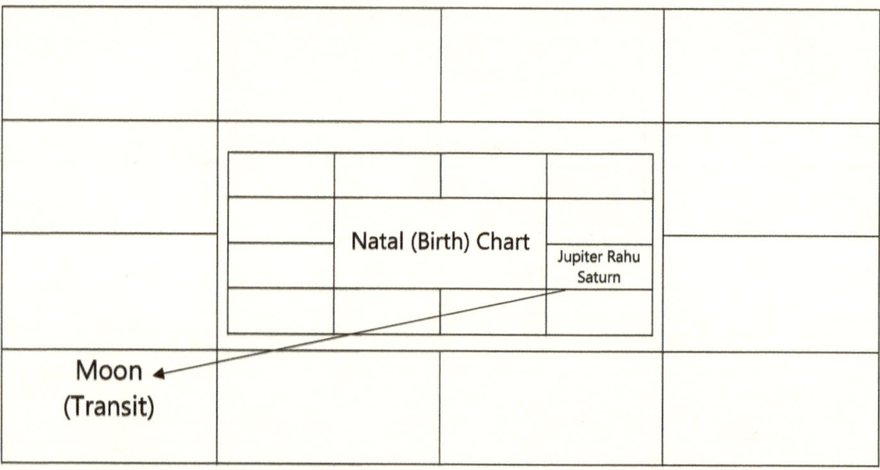

In the natal chart displayed above, Jupiter in Leo is caught between malefic Rahu and Saturn losing all its beneficial powers thereby acting indifferently.

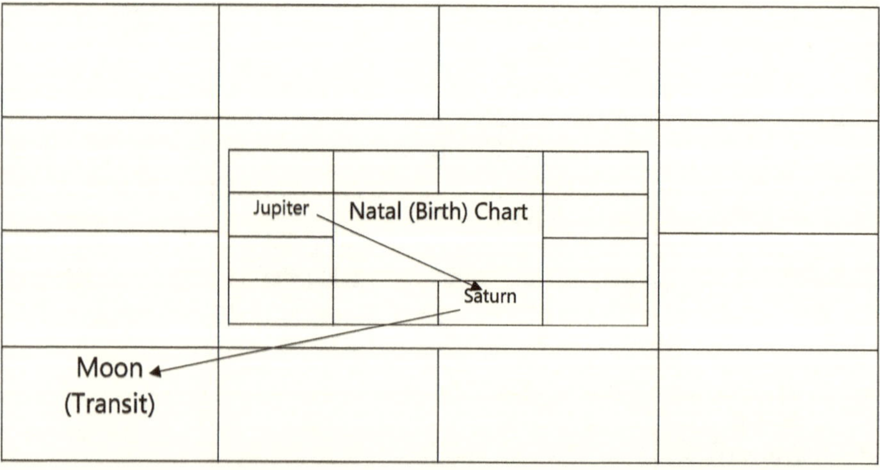

Please note from the above natal (birth) chart, that exalted Saturn in Libra receives the 9th aspect of Jupiter in Aquarius (Saturn's house) raising its powers to 500%. Saturn transforms this 500% beneficial power to the transit Moon in Sagittarius through its 3rd aspect doing all good.

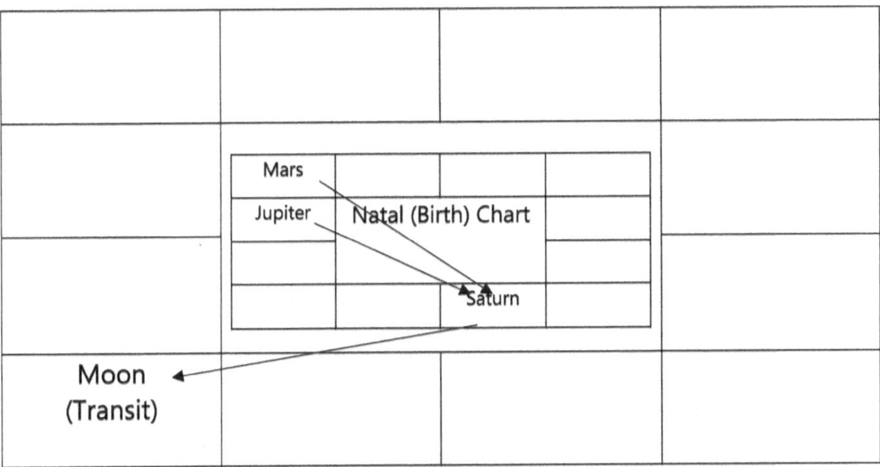

In the above natal (birth) chart, exalted Saturn in Libra is in receipt of the 8th aspect of malefic Mars from Pisces and the 9th aspect of beneficial Jupiter from Aquarius thereby acquiring mixed fortunes. Hence, the exalted

Saturn in Libra transforms the mixed results of good and bad fortunes to the transit Moon through its 3rd aspect.

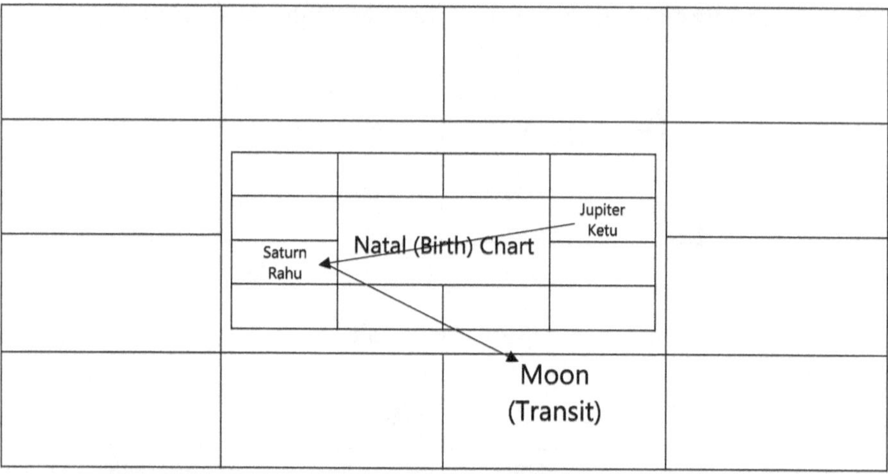

The above natal (birth) chart is considered cruel as natal Saturn in Capricorn is associated with Rahu and receipt of the 7th aspect of natal Jupiter with Ketu in Cancer. The conjunction of Ketu with Jupiter pushes the native to borrow heavily. To pay off the loans, the natives accepted bribes and were caught in corruption cases. The combined aspect of Rahu and Saturn falls on the transit Moon confirming jail sentence to the native as Rahu is the significator of corruption and illegal activities. Here, Jupiter involves huge money through borrowings as he is associated with Ketu, a significator of debt and law enforcement. The confinement term in jail will be long if the Maha Dasa (Dasa), and Anthar Dasa (Bukthi) signify the query being unfavourable and will be temporary or lasting till the end of the transit period.

Significance of 'Chandra Naadi' – Certain Examples

Example: 1

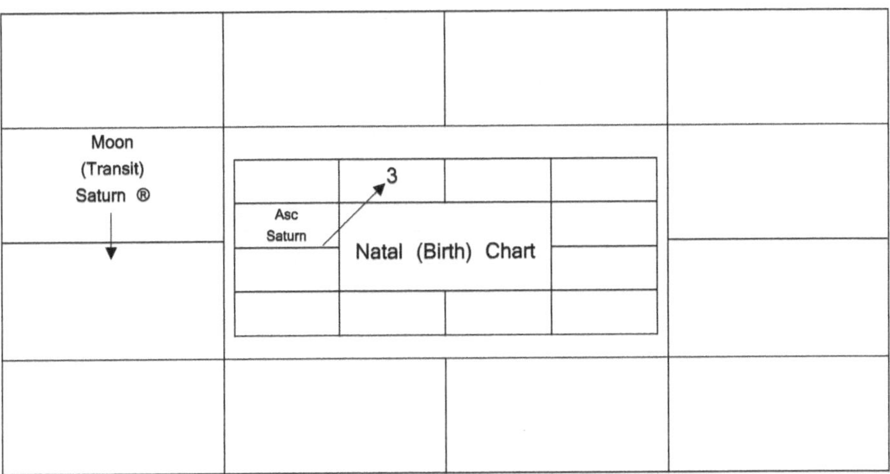

In the above natal (birth) chart, the transit Moon is entering into Aquarius and about to touch the Saturn posited there. Hence the probable questions as indicated by 'Chandra Naadi' may be about 1) Job 2) Fear of Life 3) Ancestral property or family God.

The native is currently running Venus Maha Dasa (Dasa) of the 4th and 9th house.

The transit Saturn in Aquarius is in retrograde motion moving towards the 12th house Capricorn. This indicates the native's inclination to move to other states or foreign countries to take up a job. It will relieve the natives from the fear of Life.

Though the Maha Dasa (Dasa) in operation is Venus – that of the Kalathra (life partner) Karaka – the transit Moon has no connection to Venus devoid of Marriage prospects.

Example: 2

<table>
<tr><td colspan="4"></td></tr>
<tr><td rowspan="2">Moon
(Transit)</td><td colspan="2">
<table>
<tr><td></td><td>3</td><td></td><td></td></tr>
<tr><td>Asc Saturn◄</td><td colspan="3" align="right">Mars</td></tr>
<tr><td></td><td colspan="2" align="center">Natal (Birth) Chart</td><td></td></tr>
<tr><td></td><td>10</td><td></td><td></td></tr>
</table>
</td><td></td></tr>
<tr><td></td></tr>
<tr><td colspan="4"></td></tr>
</table>

In the above natal (birth) chart having Aquarius ascendant, the ascendant lord is posited in its own ruling house. Mars is the lord of the 3rd and the 10th house signifying business posited in the 6th house in debilitated condition ruling out any possibility of business prospects. The other Karakathuvas of Mars like buying land and buildings are also ruled out. It indicates that the native will be accident-prone.

The Transit of Moon over Rahu – Results through 'Chandra Naadi'

Example: 3

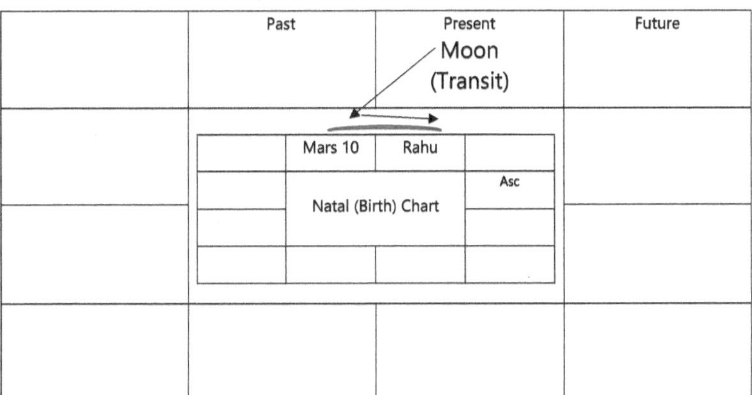

In the above Cancer Ascendant natal (birth) chart, Mars in Aries possesses directional 10th house strength and the natively is currently running Mars Maha Dasa (Dasa) and Rahu Prityanthar Dasa (Antharam). As Mars is considered the lord of fortunes and running favourable Mars Maha Dasa (Dasa), the native was under the impression that he would have undue fortunes. But according to 'Chandra Naadi' the presentation is something else.

As per 'Chandra Naadi', the transit Moon has surpassed the natal Mars in Aries and is moving towards natal Rahu in Taurus. Hence, only the impact of Rahu and its Karakathuvas like surgery, problems, and litigation will impact the native instead of his fortune expectations.

Example: 1

A firm's proprietress approached me with her natal (birth) chart for consultation. At that time, the transit Moon was passing over Leo receiving the aspect of natal (birth) Saturn posited with Mars in Gemini in her natal (birth) chart.

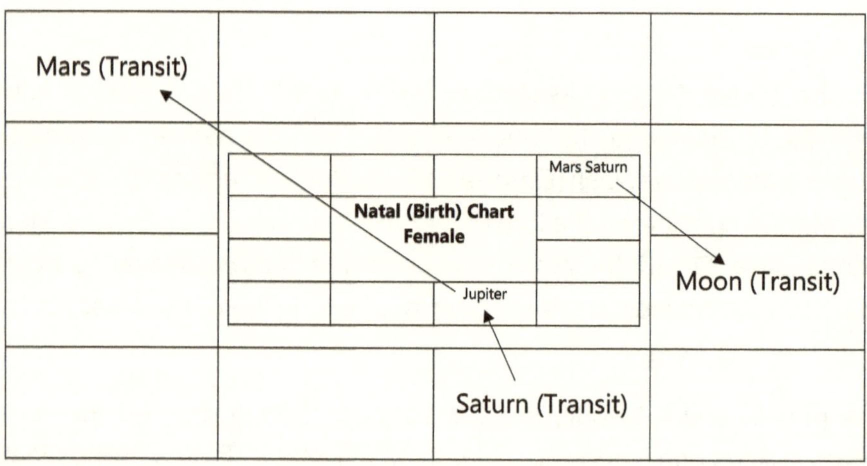

I told her that she could purchase new machinery, add additional types of machinery and increase the size of the buildings which would not face any hurdles.

She affirmed with a smile that her approach is to ask about the same by adding adjacent buildings to accommodate two more machines.

As the transit Saturn in Libra is passing over natal (birth) Jupiter in the same Libra and its aspect of the transit Mars in Pisces – the significator of Machines and buildings, I advised her to proceed immediately.

Example: 2

Given below is another natal (birth) chart which has natal (birth) Saturn in Libra and the transit Moon passing over it (in Libra). The natal Jupiter associated with the Ketu throws its 5th aspect over the transit Moon in Libra.

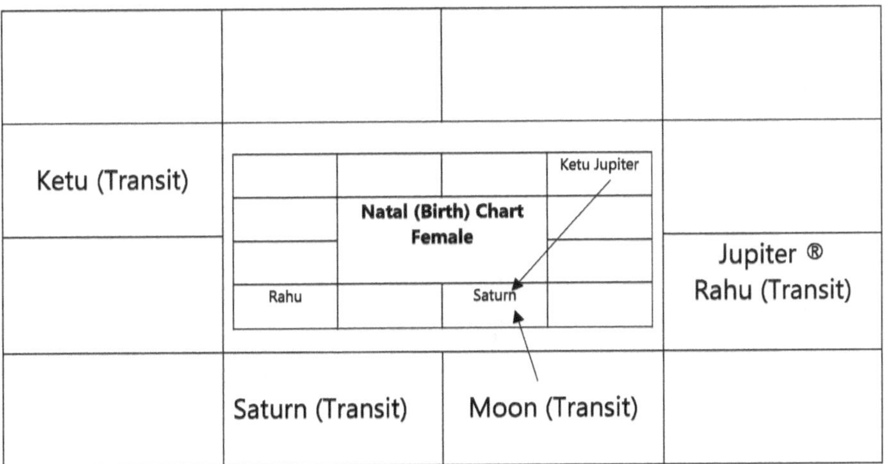

I asked the querist whether the query Was about business and loan requirements for the same or

It's about his son's welfare, his marriage prospects, and his business.

The querist confirmed his intention about the same.

As Saturn indicates Job/Business and Ketu conjoined with Jupiter denotes the loan requirements. In Transit, the conjunction of retrograde Jupiter with Rahu in Leo denies the availability of a loan.

The prospective income dues and non-availability of a loan will delay all auspicious events planned for his son.

He was suggested to be patient till the passing of transit Jupiter over transit Rahu and become direct as his monetary requirements will be fulfilled after that.

He called up a day after Jupiter became direct to inform me that he had received loans from both sources.

He was told to concentrate on his business which will flourish hereafter.

Ketu conjoined Jupiter and pushed the native not only into the debt trap but also forbade happy occasions in the family.

At times even auspicious events are carried out secretly.

Example: 3

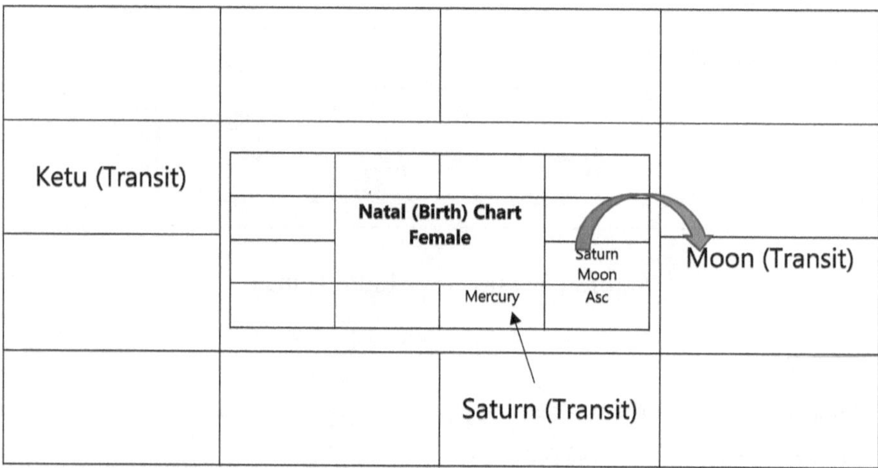

The querist is a middle-aged man, who has his transit Moon passing over the natal(birth) chart Saturn + Moon in Leo.

I told him that he is presently suffering from losses in his hotel business and the loss will continue. He was also cautioned not to venture into self-employment.

But the querist replied that he is not interested in any business other than hotels and not willing to go for any employment. Saturn + Moon combination in his natal (birth) chart compels him to venture into the food business and he is currently running the Maha Dasa (Dasa) of the 4th house lord, it will help him for the time being if he runs the hotel with a partner with less investment. When the investment grows, there will be a betrayal involving funds.

As the transit Saturn is moving over Mercury in Libra – the significator of partners/associates – it will bring good fortunes as long as no greed exists.

Example: 4

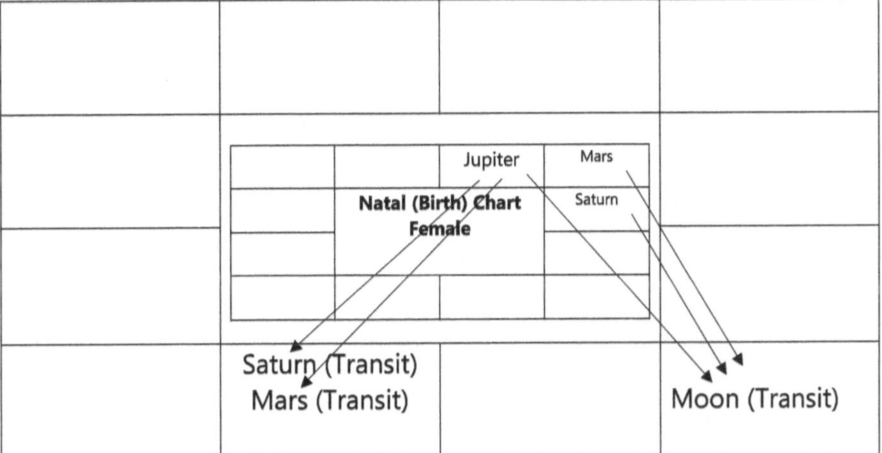

The querist of the above natal (birth) chart approached and sat before me tight-lipped as if he wanted to know everything through me.

I told him that he could venture into the real estate business on a large scale but had to wait a long time to reap the profit. The money will get locked up and will take a few years to return manyfold.

The querist wanted to make sure about doing real estate business and prepared to wait to get the return of money invested.

He was told that as both transit Mars and transit Saturn are under the aspect of natal (Birth) Jupiter, success in the real estate business is assured.

Virgo and Real Estate Business...

Of the three signs Taurus, Virgo, and Capricorn representing one of the primordial lands, Virgo is the most important and most beneficial than the other two.

When Mars is posited in Virgo or aspect the sign Virgo, the native will be engaged in the real estate business bringing fame and good income through land.

A real estate venture is probable if Saturn associates or conjoins Mars connected to the signs representing land (Taurus, Virgo, Capricorn).

The combination of Saturn + Mars + Mercury will facilitate the real estate business.

When Virgo becomes the 2nd, 10th, or 11th house to the native's ascendant, it gives rise to the real estate business.

The Moon + Mars + Mercury + Saturn association will also be a venture in the real estate business.

The movement of the transit Moon concerning natal (birth) Mars and natal (birth) Saturn is ideally the best time to talk about the real estate business with the querist.

Example: 5

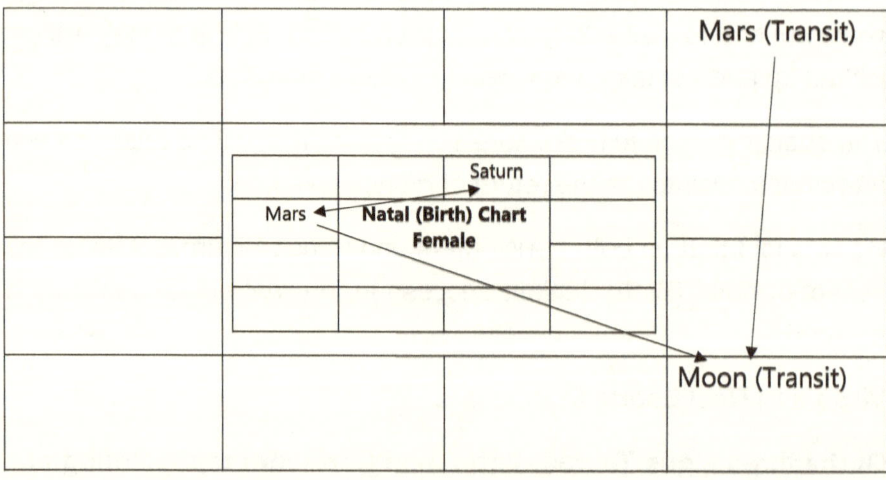

The transit Moon is traversing in Virgo and the native is currently running Saturn Maha Dasa (Dasa), Saturn Anthar Dasa (Bukthi), and Mars Prityanthar Dasa (Antharam).

As the transit Moon receives the natal (Birth) Mars's aspect, the current transit position of Mars should be reckoned.

The transit Mars in Gemini throws its 4th aspect over Virgo where the transit Moon is in motion. The native is into the real estate business and she was worried about a huge investment made. I told her to close the deal somehow even at the cost of lesser profit as the Mars Prityanthar Dasa (Antharam) is about to end in another 20 days failing which it will take a few more years to sell the property and realise her money.

She returned after a few days to inform me that he closed the deal and realised money close to 1 Crore.

Rahu/Ketu in Virgo Destroys Real Estate Business

Example: 6

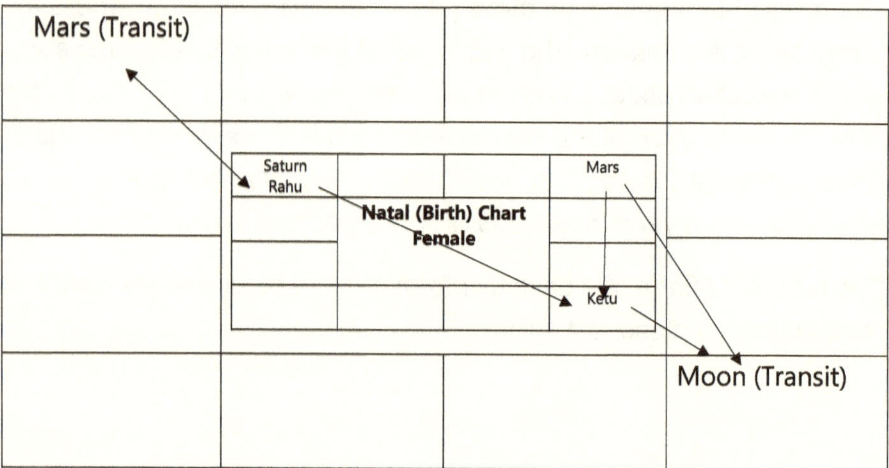

In the above natal (birth) chart Saturn and Rahu are in Pisces and Mrs in Gemini. The combined aspect of Saturn and Mars falls on Ketu posited in Virgo over which the transit Virgo Moon passes over.

I have instructed the above native not to venture into the real estate business but he teased me saying that he is interested only in the real estate business.

When transit Mars was in Pisces, he suffered heavy losses in the real estate business and went into hiding. His interest in the real estate business was triggered by the aspect of both Saturn from Pisces and Mars from Gemini.

He suffered heavy losses due to the presence of Ketu in Virgo and Saturn's association with the destroyer Rahu in Pisces where the transit Mars traversed causing loss and disgrace in the real estate business.

It is construed that the real estate business is forbidden if the nodes Rahu or Ketu are present in the Virgo Sign.

Example: 7

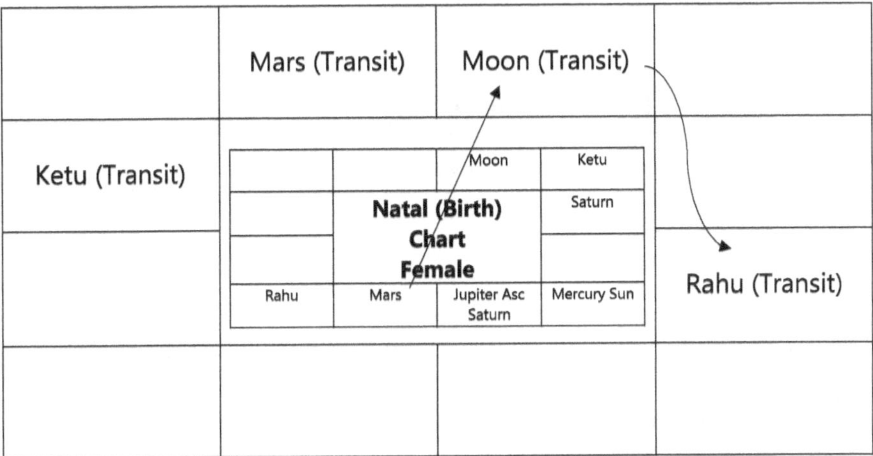

In the above natal (birth) chart, the transit Moon passes over the natal (birth) Moon which gets the 7th aspect of natal (Birth) Mars in Scorpio.

I told her that she intended to know about some landed property and her health as intuited by 'Chandra Naadi'. She confirmed it.

As the Moon initiates all changes, she would like to change the place of business and look for a better alternative.

She was advised not to make any changes as the planets that are in touch with the transit Moon do not form any part of the Maha Dasa (Dasa), Anthar Dasa (Bukthi), or the Prityanthar Dasa (Antharam) running currently indirectly indicating heavy loss if any changed are attempted to. As there are no planets in between natal (birth) Capricorn Sign to Taurus, the native survives without any changes and the movement of the transit Moon towards transit Rahu in Leo will result in significant losses as it is a malefic planet. Had there been any beneficial planets like Jupiter or Venus, the intended change could bring beneficial results.

Example: 8

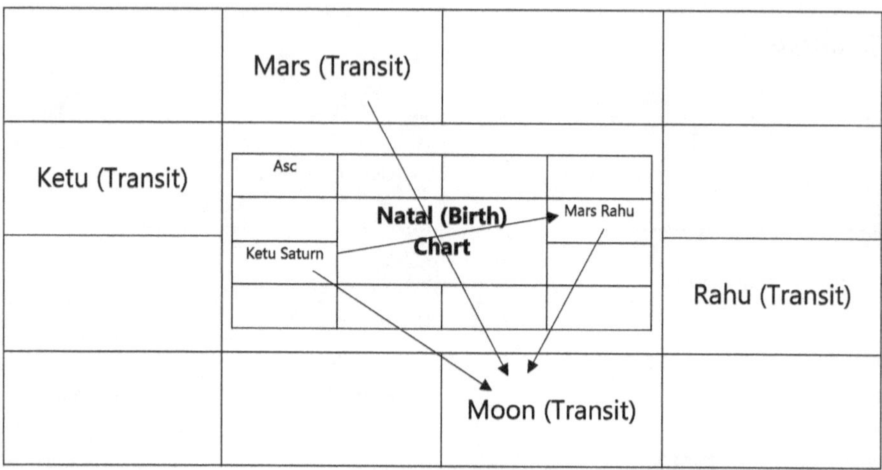

In the above natal (birth) chart, natal Mars and Rahu are in Cancer and Saturn is placed in Capricorn along with Ketu. As per our 'Chandra Naadi' rules about the planets that are closely connected to the transit Moon, in this transit position, the transit Mars and natal Mars aspect the transit Moon through their 4th aspect and 7th aspect respectively.

I asked the querist whether he would like to ask about house and land, and he replied in affirmative. Further, his question was about buying an old house, demolishing it and constructing newly. I told him to proceed.

How was the prediction done?

1. The natal Cancer Mars is under the aspect of Ruling Saturn in Capricorn defining it as an older one.
2. As both Saturn and Mars are associated with the nodes Rahu and Ketu, demolition of the house is suggested.
3. Rahu and Ketu represent Chisel – a tool used to break.
4. Saturn is the Karaka for breaking.
5. Mars is the Karaka for the house.

As the transit Mars is more powerfully positioned than the natal Mars, the native is presently in a position to build a house than at birth.

The natal Mars is in debilitation and placed with Rahu displaying the native's weak position during birth while the same is positioned strongly during the current transit of Mars facilitating the Karakathuvas of Mars temporarily exhibiting the difference of natal and transit position of the same planet.

Example: 9

In the below Libra ascendant natal chart, Moon, Mercury and Saturn are posited in the 12th house and the transit Moon is moving over them in Virgo.

The transit Moon has crossed the natal Moon and natal Mercury degree-wise positions and approaching natal Saturn.

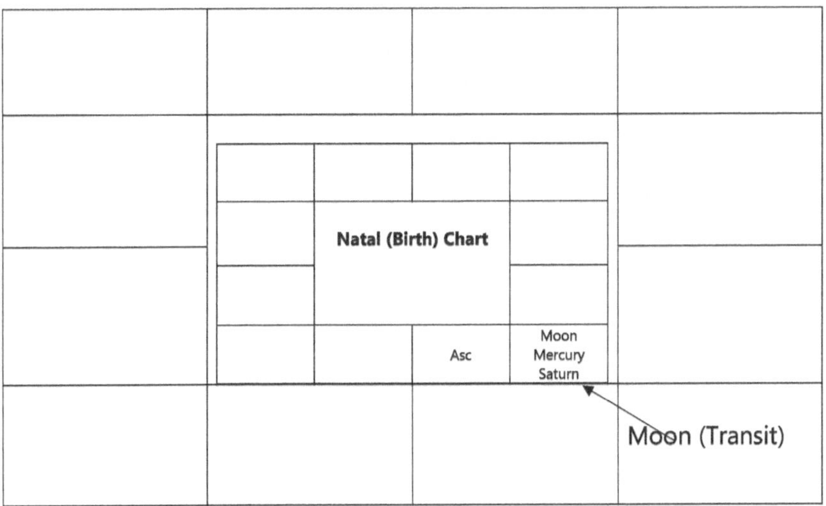

When the native of the above natal (birth) chart approached me, I told him that his self-employment would end in loss and getting cheated by many. He was advised to engage himself in job work.

The native replied about his loss and betrayal by his friends but received a call again to start the business on a partnership basis.

As the transit Moon is traversing in the 12th house from the ascendant, it will again face the same bitterness and failure in partnership thus liquidating the remaining financial assets. He was strongly advised not to venture into partnership.

Why did he get a call again for a partnership business?

As the transit Moon is connecting with the natal Moon, Mercury, and Saturn, it revives the old events.

What prompted the native to look for self-employment and face losses?

The conjunction of the Moon and Saturn prompted the natives to go for self-employment and their placement in the 12th house caused the dissipation/loss.

Is there any other way to carry on business on a partnership basis by those with the above Saturn + Moon combination?

Those with a Saturn + Moon combination in the 12th house can join as working partners and receive a sum on a monthly or weekly basis for the service rendered. They should stop instigating others which will not hinder the progress of the business.

Example: 10

A querist approached me to check marital compatibility with his natal (birth) chart. The transit Moon was passing over the natal (birth) Rahu and the native is currently running Rahu Maha Dasa (Dasa).

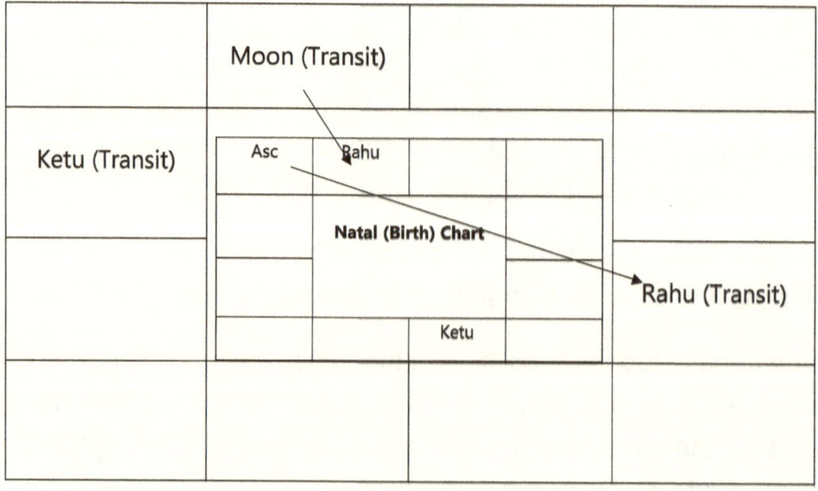

As the transit Moon passes over the natal (birth) Rahu, the transit Rahu's position should be reckoned to compute the results.

As the transit Rahu is in the crucial 6th house from Pisces Ascendant, the marital compatibility will not arise and the confirmation of the same may be seen from the natal (birth) chart of the other person who will run Rahu Maha Dasa (Dasa), Rahu Anthar Dasa (Bukthi) or the asterism of Rahu.

The other person was running Rahu Maha Dasa (Dasa).

Both the parties concerned were about to fix the marriage date causing a dilemma in me.

After a few months, they met me to inform me that the marriage did not take place owing to some loose talk by some family friend on the bride's side.

Rahu causes anxiety, terror and gossip through which it nips a union.

The gossip created fear in the minds of all the concerned. The currency of Rahu Maha Dasa (Dasa) and the transit of Rahu's position in the 6th house to the natal (birth) Pisces ascendant hindered the progress of an auspicious event.

They were assured of the marriage to somebody else as Rahu is placed in the 2nd house (Family) to the ascendant.

Example: 11

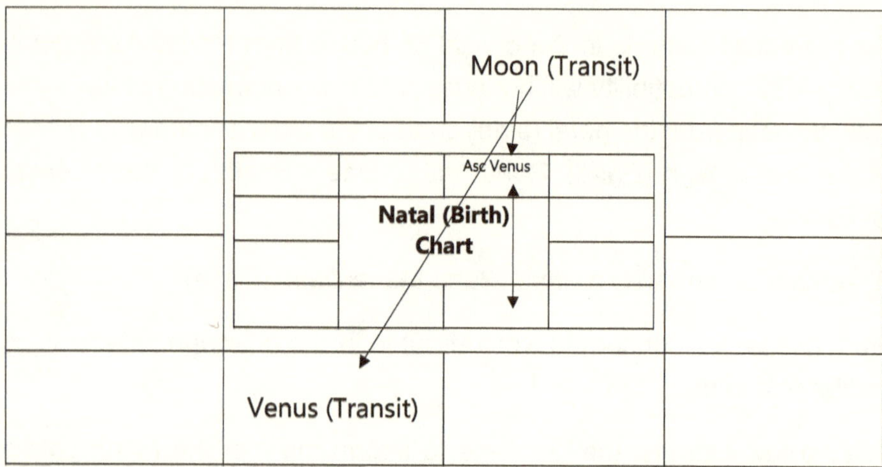

The above querist is born in Taurus ascendant with Venus posited in it. He approached me on the day of the transit of the Moon over natal (birth) Taurus Venus and the transit Venus moving in Scorpio.

I asked them whether they intended to consult for their financial requirements and got it confirmed to them.

After a brief analysis, I construed that they require money for medical expenses as they might be suffering either from uterus problems or Kidney problems forcing medical treatment and asked them whether their financial requirements are towards medical treatment.

They affirmed it by saying that they were suffering from uterine fibroid that required surgery and were left with no money to meet the expenses.

They were advised to carry out the surgery at the earliest.

The Prediction Process:

For the Taurus ascendant, Venus is the lord of the ascendant and lord of the 6th house owning dual lordship.

The Transit Moon passes over the lord of the 6th house in Taurus thereby confirming the affliction by disease.

As Venus, the lord of the 6th is transiting over Scorpio, problems relating to the uterus urinary tract, and Kidney are subjected to damage.

As the transit Moon is over Venus, the need for money – another Karaka – of Venus is highlighted.

Example: 12

Below displayed is that of a native who has a Gemini Ascendant with Mars in Leo.

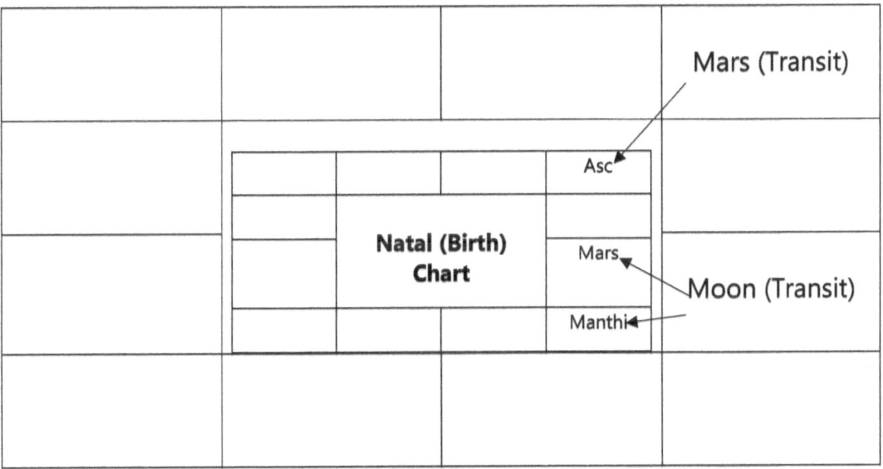

The transit Moon passes over the 6th house lord Mars to Gemini ascendant and the 6th house lord Mars is moving over the Gemini ascendant. The native is currently running Mars Maha Dasa (Dasa).

The natives will be suffering from serious diseases. The position of Mars in Leo signifies severe affliction of the abdomen and Kidney.

The reduced blood level makes the native anaemic and inflammation of the body. He was advised to consult a specialist immediately.

He inquired whether his death was nearing. Indeed, it is. As the transit Moon was about to touch Manthi in the next square, he was cautioned.

He died due to Kidney failure after a few days. The transit Moon that was about to touch Manthi indicated his end.

Example: 13

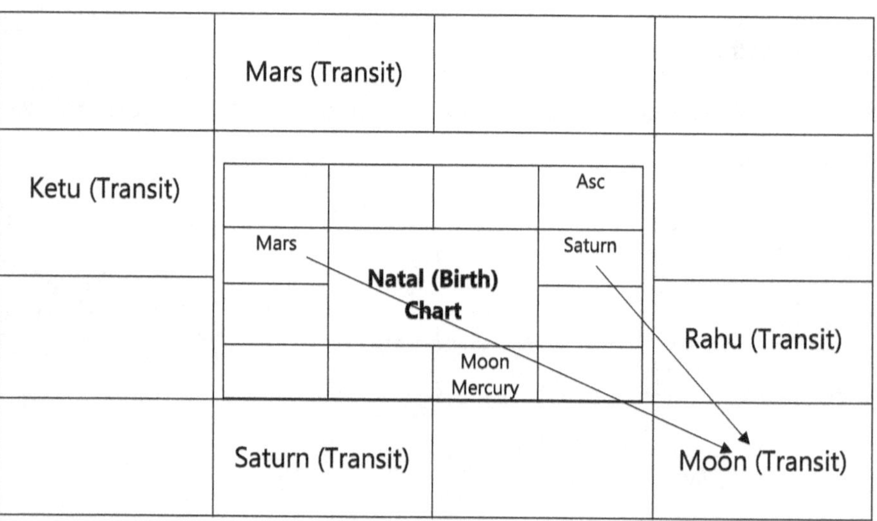

The above natal (birth) chart is that of a native who has Gemini as ascendant, Saturn in Cancer and Mars in Aquarius. Both natal Saturn's 3rd aspect and the 8th aspect of natal Mars fall on the transit Moon.

The natal Saturn is traversing in the 6th house Scorpio in transit and Aquarius Ketu is transiting over natal Mars.

When the native approached for consultation, he was told that he would have borrowed for his business and he should up his efforts to liquidate the loan failing which legal actions would be initiated against him by his lenders'.

The native acknowledged my information and expressed his inability to find the source for the same.

As the natal Moon and Mercury are posited in Libra, it will be ideal to get property documents from the mother and repay the loans by pledging them in the Banks. It will help him to restart his business and get relieved from the borrowings in full.

Gemini ascendants are prone to debts and diseases more than any other ascendants, It is due to their over-expectations and actions without any proper planning.

Next to Gemini ascendant, Virgo and Scorpio are the most affected by debts.

For Martian ascendants (Aries and Scorpio) Mercury Maha Dasa (Dasa) and Mercurian ascendants (Gemini and Virgo) Mars Maha Dasa (Dasa) are cruel in extending unexhaustive debts, chronic and constant diseases along with unbearable distress.

Financial Gains Through the House and Landed Properties

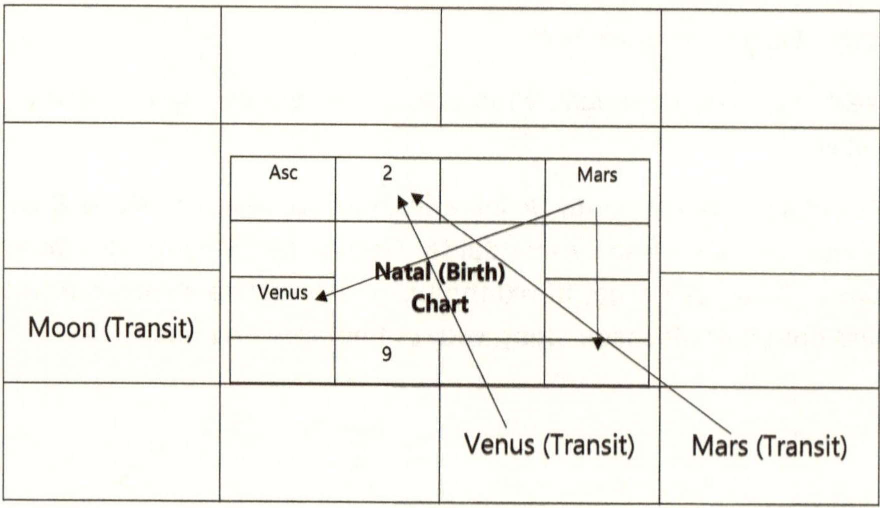

In the above-displayed natal (birth) Pisces ascendant chart, natal Venus in Capricorn receives the 8th aspect of natal (birth) Mars from Gemini whereas the transit Moon is passing over it.

As per our 'Chandra Naadi' rules, the query will be a mixture of the Bhavaga, and Karakathuvas of both Mars and Venus put together.

The results should be declared based on the transit of Mars and Venus.

The natal (birth) Mars posited in 4th house Gemini from Pisces ascendant throws its 4th aspect on Virgo – the significator of fortunes through the land – and 8th aspect on natal Venus – the significator of money.

The transit Mars passes through Virgo and the transit Venus moves through Libra – both throwing their aspect on 2nd house Aries representing income sources.

The querist was informed about his expectations of money through the house and landed properties. He was astonished at my results and wanted to know how I made the predictions. That is the excellence of 'Chandra Naadi'.

How was it Judged?

We know that Venus signifies money, but the aspect of Mars over it indicates that the money will be through the Karakathuvas of Mars.

While Venus posited alone indicates money, its association or connection with Mars shows that it is through one of the Karakathuvas of Mars who is posited in the 4th bhavaga from Pisces ascendant pointing at the house and landed properties.

Though a planet possesses multiple Karakathuvas, when the results are declared by correlating with the Bhavaga and identifying it will add more value to predictions made.

-The End-

Ohm Sree Uchishta Maha Ganapathaye Namah: